HANDBOOK
SERIES
BOOK 5

How to Manage the Blue Orchard Bee

As an Orchard Pollinator

Jordi Bosch and William P. Kemp

Sustainable Agriculture Network
National Agricultural Library
Beltsville, MD 20705-2351

A publication of the Sustainable Agricultural Network with funding by the
USDA-ARS Bee Biology and Systematics Laboratory, Logan, Utah, and the
USDA-CSREES Sustainable Agriculture Research and Education (SARE) program.

Line drawings by G. Frehner. Cover photo by D.F. Veirs. Cover inset by USDA-ARS. Photographs by J. Bosch (Figures 1, 19, and 45); J. H. Cane (Figure 43); W. P. Kemp (Figure 2); G. Neuenswander (Figures 3, 5, 8, 10, 11, 14–18, 20-23, 36-38, 40, 46, 51, and 53); USDA-ARS (Figure 13); USU Photo Services (Figure 25); and D. F. Veirs (Figures 7, 9, 12, 26, 30–35, 39, 41, 42, 44, 47–50, 55, and 57).

Printed in 2001 by the Sustainable Agriculture Network (SAN), with funding from the Sustainable Agriculture Research and Education (SARE) program of the CSREES, U.S. Department of Agriculture. This book was supported by funds of USDA-CSREES project award no. 2001-48546-01236. Contact SAN before reproducing any part of this book.

SAN is the national outreach arm of USDA's SARE program. Since 1988, SARE has worked to advance farming systems that are profitable, environmentally sound and good for communities. For more information about SAN and SARE, see www.sare.org or contact:

SAN Coordinator
National Agricultural Library, Room 124
10301 Baltimore Ave.
Beltsville, MD 20705-2351
(301) 504-6422; (301) 504-6927(fax)
san@nal.usda.gov

Material for this book was researched and written by the Bee Biology & Systematics Laboratory of USDA's Agricultural Research Service. The book format was developed under the auspices of the Sustainable Agriculture Network.

To order copies of this book ($9.95 plus $3.95 s/h) contact (802) 656-0484 or sanpubs@uvm.edu

Library of Congress Cataloging-in-Publication Data

Bosch, Jordi, 1961-
  How to manage the blue orchard bee as an orchard pollinator / Jordi Bosch and William Kemp.
    p. cm – (Sustainable Agriculture Network handbook series ; bk. 5)
  Includes bibliographical references (p.).
  ISBN 1-888626-06-2 (pbk.)
   1. Orchard mason bee. I. Kemp, William P. (William Paul) II. Title. III. Series.

SF539.8.O73 B67 2001
638'.1-dc21

2001055135

This text is intended to be a guide, and should be used in conjunction with other information sources on farm and orchard management. The editor, authors and publisher disclaim any liability, loss, or risk, personal or otherwise, which is incurred as a consequence, directly or indirectly, of the use and application of any of the contents of this book.

Mention, visual representation or inferred reference of a product, service, manufacturer or organization in this publication does not imply endorsement by the USDA, the SARE program or the authors. Exclusion does not imply a negative evaluation.

Graphic design, interior layout and cover design by Andrea Gray. Block art by Bonnie Acker. Printing by Jarboe Printing, Washington, D.C.

Contents

Acknowledgments v

Preface vi

1 **FRUIT TREE POLLINATION** 1

2 **THE BLUE ORCHARD BEE** 4
   2.1 Mating and Nesting 5
   2.2 Life Cycle 9
   2.3 Foraging Behavior and Pollinating Efficacy 12

3 **ARTIFICIAL NESTING MATERIALS** 16
   3.1 Types of Nesting Materials 16
   3.2 Cavity Dimensions 20

4 **HOW TO REAR BOB POPULATIONS** 22
   4.1 Nesting 23
   4.2 Development, Pre-wintering, and Wintering 25
   4.3 Incubation and Emergence 32

5 **HOW TO RELEASE BOB POPULATIONS IN ORCHARDS** 35
   5.1 Timing BOB Emergence with Orchard Bloom 35
   5.2 Release Methods 37

    5.3 Bees per Acre   38

    5.4 Advancing Emergence for Almond Pollination   39

6 OTHER MANAGEMENT PRACTICES   41

    6.1 Providing Alternative Pollen-Nectar Sources   41

    6.2 Moving Active BOB Populations   42

7 FACTORS LIMITING BOB POPULATION GROWTH   44

    7.1 Pre-nesting Female Dispersal   44

    7.2 Pesticide Sprays   45

    7.3 Developmental and Winter Mortality   46

8 PARASITES, PREDATORS, AND PATHOGENS   49

    8.1 Chalcid Wasps, *Monodontomerus* spp.   49

    8.2 Chalcid Wasp, *Melittobia chalybii*   51

    8.3 Chalcid Wasp, *Leucospis affinis*   53

    8.4. Chrysidid Wasps, *Chrysura* spp.   54

    8.5 Sapygid Wasp, *Sapyga* sp.   54

    8.6 Cuckoo Bee, *Stelis montana*   55

    8.7 Blister Beetle, *Tricrania stansburyi*   56

    8.8 Checkered Flower Beetle, *Trichodes ornatus*   57

    8.9 Spider Beetle, *Ptinus californicus*   58

    8.10 Carpet Beetles, Dermestidae   59

    8.11 Flour Beetles, *Tribolium* spp.   59

    8.12 Hairy-fingered Mite, *Chaetodactylus krombeini*   59

    8.13 Chalkbrood, *Ascosphaera* spp.   62

    8.14 Birds, Rodents, and Ants   63

9 HOW TO QUANTIFY BOB POPULATIONS   65

10 HOW TO OBTAIN BOB POPULATIONS   67

    10.1 Trap-nesting BOBs   67

    10.2 Purchasing BOBs   69

11 CONCLUDING REMARKS   71

    Appendix   74

    Bibliography   78

    Index   85

Acknowledgments

WE WOULD LIKE TO EXPRESS our sincere appreciation to Phil Torchio, without whose extensive work and creative insights the blue orchard bee would continue to be just one of many other wild bee species. As for our own research, we are indebted to Glen Trostle for his essential and continuing contributions, as well as Shaila Kalaskar and Peggy Rieger for their outstanding field and laboratory work. Don Veirs was very generous with his time, patience, and photography skills. We also thank Jack Neff (Central Texas Melittological Institute, Austin, Texas) for providing blue orchard bee nests from Texas, and Eric Grissell (USDA-ARS, Washington, D.C.) and Barry O'Connor (University of Michigan, Ann Arbor, Michigan) for information on parasitoid and mite taxonomy, respectively. Mary Barkworth (Intermountain Herbarium, Logan, Utah) reviewed the common and scientific names of plants. This manuscript was improved through important suggestions from Jim Cane (USDA-ARS, Logan, Utah), Chet Kendell (Kendell Orchards, North Ogden, Utah), Yasuo Maeta (Tottori University, Tottori, Japan), Steve Peterson (IPS, Visalia, California), Evan Sugden (Entomo-Logic, SE Monroe, Washington), Phil Torchio (USDA-ARS, Logan, Utah [retired]), Joe Traynor (Scientific Ag Co., Bakersfield, California), and Glen Trostle (USDA-ARS, Logan, Utah). Lastly, we appreciate the editorial and production efforts of SAN staff, Valerie Berton and Andy Clark, as well as the design work of Andrea Gray.

Preface

THE WORLDWIDE POLLINATION of insect-pollinated crops has traditionally depended on a single species, the honey bee (*Apis mellifera*), for many decades the only pollinator available commercially in large numbers. The risks of relying on a single species are obvious.

First, shortages in available populations in any given year or geographical area may jeopardize pollination, and hence production, in a large section of crops. In the past decade, the number of honey bee hives available for commercial pollination in the United States has seriously declined, mostly due to low honey prices and the introduction of parasitic mites and other exotic honey bee pests. Second, honey bees do not readily visit or effectively pollinate certain cultivated plants.

For those reasons, other pollinator species have been developed for particular crops around the world. Commercially managed pollinators include the alkali bee (*Nomia melanderi*), the gray-haired alfalfa bee (*Rhophitoides canus*), the alfalfa leafcutting bee (*Megachile rotundata*), several bumblebee species (*Bombus* spp.), and several mason bee species (*Osmia* spp.).

The blue orchard bee, *Osmia lignaria*, native to North America, has been developed as a pollinator for orchard crops. It is also known as the orchard mason bee because it uses mud to build its nests. The blue orchard bee is a close relative of the hornfaced bee, *Osmia cornifrons*, a species that has been used as a commercial apple and cherry pollinator in Japan since the 1960s and is currently used on 75 percent of Japan's apple acreage. Another closely related species, the horned bee, *Osmia cornuta*, has been developed as an orchard pollinator in Europe.

Most of the pioneering research on the biology and management of the blue orchard bee, starting in the 1970s, was conducted by Phil Torchio of the USDA-ARS Bee Biology and Systematics Laboratory, in Logan, Utah. Research on the blue orchard bee and the delivery of management systems tailored for specific crops continues, mainly through our own studies. With blue orchard bees becoming commercially available in North America, the Bee Biology and Systematics Laboratory receives frequent inquiries about managing this species for pollination of fruit trees and other crops. Many of these inquiries come from growers interested in using the new pollinator in their orchards and from beekeepers who want to diversify their pollination services. Other inquiries come from gardeners interested in having a non-aggressive pollinator in their back yards, or from schoolteachers and students who would like to use this easy-to-rear and fascinating bee in their science projects.

Information on the biology and management of the blue orchard bee is mostly restricted to scientific publications. In this manual, we review and synthesize that information and present it in a way that is readily useable by those interested in managing blue orchard bee populations for fruit tree pollination. We also hope the manual will interest bee researchers and help identify areas of knowledge needing further investigation.

Many of the blue orchard bee management activities are not yet standardized. Our intent is to upgrade this review as ongoing research provides new information, and the commercial establishment of the blue orchard bee (hereafter referred to as BOB) results in improved large-scale management techniques.

How to Use this Manual

How to Manage the Blue Orchard Bee as an Orchard Pollinator is organized in 11 sections. In section 1, we provide a brief overview of fruit tree pollination, in which we emphasize the importance of pollinating as many flowers as possible, as early as possible in the bloom period. In section 2, we describe the general biology of the BOB. Basic knowledge on the life cycle, nesting and foraging behavior is essential to understand the rest of the sections and successfully manage the BOB.

In the next four sections, we provide information on how to rear and manage BOB populations. In section 3, we describe a variety of nesting materials now available for rearing BOBs and emphasize the importance of using adequate cavity dimensions. Sections 4 and 5 are similar in scope, but differ in scale. In section 4, we provide a general account of how to rear BOB populations from nesting through development, wintering and emergence the following year. This section provides enough information for rearing small BOB populations to pollinate gardens and small orchards.

Those interested in rearing populations for large-scale pollination operations will find in section 5 more details on bee densities needed to achieve maximum pollination and how to synchronize BOB emergence with bloom of different crops. The information provided in these two sections is extensive — we are trying to cover a vast geographical range (most of the continental United States and southern Canada), a large number of crops with different blooming periods (from almonds in February to apples in May-June), and a variety of pollination needs (from backyard gardeners to large orchardists to BOB ranchers). However, most readers will only need to use those few management practices that best fit their particular requirements (in terms of crops, geographical area, etc.). Ways to extend the nesting period and increase progeny production in commercially managed BOB populations are discussed in section 6.

In sections 7 and 8, we describe the factors limiting BOB population growth. Section 7 describes the causes and effects of pre-nesting female dispersal and mortality during development and wintering. It also describes the limited information available on the effect of pesticide sprays on BOB populations. In section 8, we provide a description of the appearance and basic biology of the most common parasites, predators, and pathogens of the BOB. Where available, we also give information on prophylactic and control methods to reduce the incidence of these antagonists. In section 9, we explain how to assess BOB population growth, and in section 10 we provide guidelines on how to trap-nest and purchase BOBs.

We encourage gardeners, growers, and beekeepers to try to rear the BOB. We are certain that the results, in terms of fruit yields and bee returns, will surprise very many. With some experience, managing BOBs should be no more difficult than managing alfalfa leafcutting bees in North America or hornfaced bees in Japan. In fact, rearing BOBs should be no more difficult than keeping honey bees.

J. B. & W. P. K.
Logan, Utah, USA
December 2001

1
FRUIT TREE POLLINATION

Fruit trees such as almonds, apricots, plums, cherries, peaches, nectarines, pears, and apples are pollinated by insects. Of the many insects visiting fruit tree flowers, bees (including honey bees, bumblebees, and many other lesser-known kinds) are most effective at moving pollen grains from flower to flower.

However, in many areas, especially those with intensive agriculture and/or pervasive urban sprawl, wild bee and feral honey bee populations are insufficient to ensure adequate pollination in orchards. Destruction or alteration of nesting habitats, pesticide use, and the scarcity of alternative flowering plants are the main factors contributing to local wild bee population declines. Due to their reproductive biology and early flowering periods, fruit trees require particularly large and/or effective pollinator populations and, therefore, fruit tree yields are often pollination-limited.

The flowering period of most orchards lasts just two to three weeks, a period frequently punctuated by spells of inclement weather. Individual flowers are typically receptive for only a few days. When poor weather hinders pollinator activity, many flowers can go unpollinated. Cool temperatures also slow pollen germination and pollen tube growth, so if flowers are pollinated at the end of their receptive period, ovules are less likely to be fertilized before ovule degeneration. For these reasons, it is desirable to pollinate fruit tree flowers for as many days as possible, particularly early in the flowering period.

An additional complicating factor in orchard pollination is that most almond, apricot, cherry, pear, and apple cultivars are not self-fertilizing. Various inter-compatible cultivars are normally planted in different rows within an orchard. Therefore, pollinators need to transfer pollen across rows for flowers to set fruit. Furthermore, almonds and cherries, in particular, have high-bearing capacities (up to 20 to 50 percent of the flowers can produce fruit) (Figure 1). Especially in almonds, where there is no trade-off between kernel size and fruit set, it is estimated that nearly 100 percent of the flowers should be pollinated to achieve maximum fruit yields.

For other orchard crops, where the size of the fruit is affected by the number produced, requiring orchardists to thin fruit, it is still important to obtain thorough pollination as early as possible. In apples and pears, which produce flowers in whorls of 5 to 6 blossoms, the central flower in each whorl, or king blossom (Figure 2), is typically the first to open and produces a larger fruit. Chemical or manual thinning removes smaller fruits and allows larger ones to mature. With

Figure 1. Almonds can set as much as 50 percent of their flowers.

fruit size and shape related to seed number, and seed number related to the number of compatible pollen grains deposited on the flower's stigmas, it is important to ensure that king blossoms receive large amounts of compatible pollen.

For these reasons, commercial orchard pollination requires supplemental use of managed pollinators. For many decades, the honey bee was the only commercially available pollinator for orchard crops in North America. Now, two mason bee species, the native BOB and the non-native hornfaced bee, introduced from Japan in the late 1970s and early 1980s, are becoming established as commercial pollinators.

Figure 2. The king apple blossom is the first to open in each whorl and sets the largest fruit.

In what follows, we describe why the BOB should be regarded as an alternative, easily managed pollinator for orchards and gardens. With a preference for foraging on fruit tree flowers, its superior pollinating efficacy, and its ability to forage under cool and cloudy weather, the BOB consistently provides adequate fruit tree pollination — if managed correctly. Its gentleness (BOBs very seldom sting) and brief nesting period make the management of BOB populations easy and especially desirable in orchard environments faced with increased urbanization.

2

THE BLUE ORCHARD BEE

The BOB, *Osmia lignaria*, belongs to the insect Order Hymenoptera and the Family Megachilidae. Like honey bees, bumblebees, and most other bee species, BOBs build nests that they provision with pollen and nectar as food for their progeny. However, BOBs differ from honey bees and bumblebees because they are solitary, not social. Social bees live in colonies with fertile queens and unmated workers that cooperate in nest building and brood-rearing activities. Solitary bees are sometimes gregarious — that is, they may nest near one another in large numbers — but each female is fertile and builds her own nest. Among solitary bees there are no castes, and no cooperation occurs among individuals concerning nest construction or the rearing of the brood. Females lay eggs in individual cells, and larvae develop by feeding on a pollen-nectar provision deposited by the mother bee.

BOB males are about two-thirds the size of a honey bee. They are metallic dark blue, sometimes blue-green, with a distinct white hair patch on the face (Figure 3). Females are larger, about the size of a honey bee, but are more stout. Female BOBs are the same color as males, but lack the extensive white hair on the face and their antennae are slightly shorter (Figure 3). Female BOBs also have a pair of horn-like prongs, difficult to see without the aid of a magnifying lens, low on their faces (Figure 4). Female BOBs have a sting, but they rarely use it. Even when in close proximity to the nest, female BOBs are not aggressive and will not sting humans, unless they are grabbed, caught under clothing, etc. BOB stings do not remain attached to human skin and are much less painful than honey bee stings. Male BOBs do not have a sting.

Males do not participate in nest construction and provisioning; they only visit flowers to collect nectar for their own consumption. Besides collecting nectar for their own sustenance, females collect large amounts of pollen and nectar for the provisioning of their brood and, therefore, pollinate higher numbers of flowers than males. Unlike honey bees and bumblebees, which carry pollen moistened with nectar on their hind legs, female BOBs carry dry pollen in a brush of long hairs (scopa) located under the abdomen (Figure 4). Light-colored pollen loads show distinctly against the dark body on the underside of a female. BOBs strongly resemble other dark-colored *Osmia* species, but those fly later in the season when BOB nesting is declining.

The BOB occurs naturally across most of the United States. In the eastern part of North America, BOB distribution extends from Nova Scotia to Georgia and west to Michigan and Texas. In the West, the BOB has been found from southern British Columbia to southern California and eastward to South Dakota and Texas. Two distinct subspecies separated by the 100th Meridian have been described: the eastern *O. lignaria lignaria*, and the western *O. lignaria propinqua*. Intermediate forms have been found in Arizona. In mid-latitude regions, BOBs have been found in locally dense populations from sea level to 6,000 feet (1,800 m), but normally become scarce at altitudes greater than 7,000–8,000 feet (2,100–2,400 m).

2.1. Mating and Nesting

BOBs are active in early spring and produce a single generation per year. Their nesting activity starts as early as February in the lower latitudes and elevations, and as late as June in colder areas. Males emerge from the nest first and typically patrol nesting sites waiting for female emergence, which generally begins one to three days later. Newly emerged females presumably exude a short-lived scent that strongly attracts males, and many mate immediately after leaving their

Figure 3. Mating blue orchard bees. Note smaller body size and longer antennae of male (right).

natal nest. Others mate while visiting nearby flowers (Figure 3). Females may mate more than once on the day of their emergence, but mated females become progressively less attractive to males.

After mating, females wait one to two days before starting nesting activities, presumably to complete maturation of their ovaries. During this time, females typically are absent from the nesting sites. After this pre-nesting period, females actively begin looking for nesting cavities. In wild populations, BOBs usually nest in abandoned beetle burrows in dead logs and stumps. A pre-nesting female repeatedly enters and inspects numerous cavities, progressively restricting her inspection visits to a particular one. Eventually, the female displays a wide zigzagging flight in front of this cavity, signaling its selection as a nesting site. Zigzagging patterns are interpreted as orientation flights that allow the female to memorize visual landmarks that will help her locate the nest cavity. Females preferentially nest near the site from which they

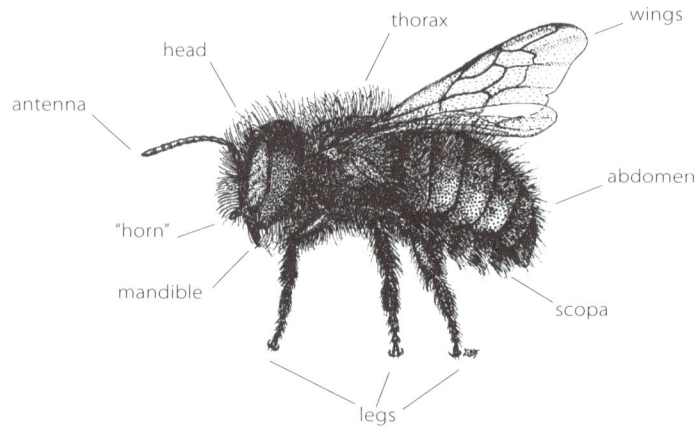

Figure 4. Main body parts of blue orchard bee adult female.

emerged, though not necessarily in the same cavity. In any population, however, some females leave the immediate area and nest elsewhere. This is referred to as pre-nesting female dispersal. Pre-nesting females are attracted to cavities adjacent to active BOB nests, a behavior that sometimes results in dense nesting aggregations.

Upon selecting a nest cavity, the female BOB starts collecting mud to build an initial partition at the deepest end of the nest cavity (Figure 5). Occasionally, the initial mud partition is built toward the middle of the nest — or skipped altogether. The BOB female gathers mud with the mandibles, shapes it into a small glob, and carries it to the nest between the mandibles and the base of the front legs. She then enters the cavity and deposits the mud, which she shapes with the mandibles. About 10 mud-collecting trips are necessary to build a complete partition. At sites with moist soil, several BOB females may simultaneously collect mud near each other.

Figure 5. Recently completed blue orchard bee nest in a reed section. The first three cells (left) contain larger pollen-nectar provisions and female eggs. Male eggs are on smaller provisions in the last four cells. Note vestibular (empty) cell and mud plug at nest entrance (right).

When the first mud partition is completed, the female BOB starts foraging for pollen and nectar to provision the first nest cell. Some 75 flower visits are necessary for a female to gather a full load of nectar and pollen. As mentioned, pollen is carried in the scopa located under the abdomen. Nectar is carried inside the bee's body, in the crop or honey stomach. Upon entering the nest, the BOB female walks to the initial partition at the bottom of the cavity and regurgitates the nectar. She then walks backwards, barely exits the nest entrance, turns around, re-enters the nest abdomen first, and backs down to the bottom of the nest. Here, she removes the pollen from her scopa using scraping movements of her hind legs, and then leaves the nest for another pollen- and nectar-collecting trip. This sequence is repeated

15 to 35 times, until a complete provision is formed. Thus, the completion of an average provision requires some 1,875 flower visits (25 loads × 75 flower visits/load). Provisions are normally shaped into a cylinder with a sloping end facing the nest entrance (Figure 5). The female BOB then makes one final flower-visiting trip, during which she collects only nectar. Upon returning to the nest, she regurgitates this nectar on the front surface (sloping end) of the provision. She then backs up and turns around at the nest entrance, re-enters abdomen first, and lays an egg on the front surface of the provision (Figure 5). After laying the egg, the female BOB carries out another series of mud-collecting trips to build a second partition that will separate the first cell from the second. Usually, mud-collecting trips take one to two minutes each, whereas pollen- and nectar-collecting trips require 10 to 15 minutes.

Cell-building, provisioning, and egg-laying continue until a linear series of adjacent cells, each with only one provision and egg, nearly fills the nest cavity (Figure 5). Then, the BOB female builds a thicker mud partition (plug or cap) at the entrance to seal the nest (Figure 5). Typically, an empty space or "vestibule" is left between the last cell constructed and the final plug. The BOB female then searches for another cavity in which to build a second nest. Nests built in six-inch (15-cm) deep cavities contain an average of five cells.

Mated females store sperm in a spermatheca, a pouch-like structure that females use to selectively fertilize eggs before oviposition. Fertilized eggs produce female progeny, and non-fertilized eggs produce male progeny. As a consequence, mated females are able to control the sex of their progeny. Although probably a rare occurrence in populations with balanced sex ratios (1.5 to 2 males per female), unmated females build nests, but will only produce male progeny. In nests built by mated females, female eggs are typically laid in the innermost cells, and male eggs in the outermost cells. Because of the larger body size of females, provisions deposited in female cells are typically larger than those deposited in male cells (Figure 5).

A nesting BOB female lives an average of 20 days and, during this time, typically provisions two to four nests. Occasionally, long-lived females may build up to seven nests. In commercial orchards, each female typically provisions two to four female cells and five to eight male cells during her lifetime. Under particularly favorable conditions, such as in greenhouses with abundant pollen-nectar resources, six nests totaling 10 female and 20 male cells per nesting female have been documented. In both field and orchard populations, the number of males is normally 1.5 to 2 times greater than the number of females. Female cells are mostly produced at the beginning of the nesting season, so early nests usually contain more female cells than late nests. Early nests also typically contain more cells than late nests.

2.2. Life Cycle

Unlike honey bees, which develop from egg to adult in 16 to 24 days, BOBs take several months to complete development (Figure 6). BOBs produce only one generation a year, and adults developing from eggs laid in spring do not emerge, mate, and nest until the spring of the following year.

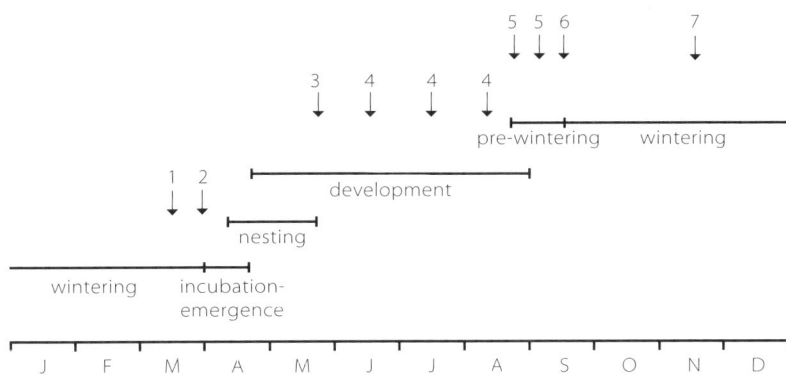

Figure 6. Life cycle and management of a late-flying (April-May) blue orchard bee population. Arrows indicate main management activities. **1**: Check emergence at room temperature (section 4.3); check fruit tree flower development and weather forecast (section 5.1). **2**: Set up nesting materials and provide mud sources (section 4.1); incubate and release population (sections 4.3, 5.1, and 5.2). **3**: Retrieve nesting materials (section 4.1) and move nests to summer storage area (section 4.2); take measures to avoid parasitism or predation (section 8). **4**: Monitor development (section 4.2). **5**: Upon adulthood, intensify development checks (section 4.2). **6**: Move nests to winter storage area (section 4.2). **7**: Quantify population and remove parasites (sections 8 and 9); prepare nesting materials for following year (section 3).

BOB eggs are white and sausage-shaped, about 0.15 inches (4 mm) long, and are attached to the pollen-nectar provision by their posterior end (Figure 5). Under field conditions, eggs require about a week to hatch. The first larval stage remains inside the egg's split chorion and feeds on egg fluids, but not on the pollen-nectar provision. Active hatching from the egg occurs only after the first larval stage molts into the second stage, which then starts feeding on the provision. Three sequential grub-like, ivory-white larval stages follow, during which the larva grows to become 0.5–0.7 inches (12–17 mm) long. The presence of small fecal pellets, approximately 0.04 inches [1 mm] long, signals the final, fifth larval stage (Figure 7). Fecal pellets are usually brown to black, rod-shaped and slightly flattened. After consuming the provision, the fifth stage larva starts spinning a cocoon of silk strands, which are produced by the salivary glands. The cocoon darkens as silk and a salivary matrix are added during the next three to four days, resulting in an opaque brown structure with a delicate silky outer layer (Figure 8). Complete cocoons are ovoid with a distinct nipple-like bump at the front end, which normally faces the nest entrance. BOB cocoons are typically attached only to the inner cell partition, leaving an empty space between the anterior tip of the cocoon and the outer cell partition (Figure 9). BOB body size is directly related to the amount of pollen-nectar provision consumed by the larva. Typical female cocoons measure 0.5–0.6 inches (12–14 mm) in length, and male cocoons 0.4–0.5 inches (10–12 mm) (Figures 8–9). However, cocoon (and body) size vary substantially, depending on weather, pollen-nectar availability, and nest cavity diameter.

Figure 7. Fifth instar blue orchard bee larva feeding on provision. Note dark fecal pellets on larva's body.

Figure 8. Male (left) and female blue orchard bee cocoons. Note nipple surrounded by white silk (foreground) and dark fecal pellets attached to cocoon walls.

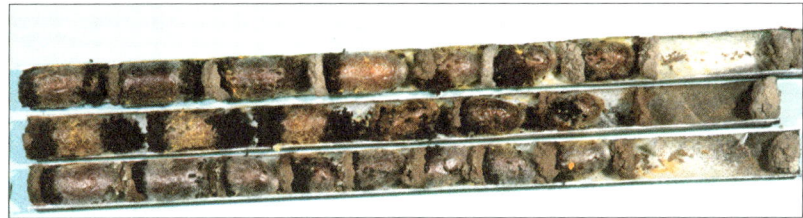

Figure 9. Three blue orchard bee nests with cocoons in paper straws. Nest entrances with vestibular cells and mud plugs are to the right. Note large female cocoons in innermost cells (left) and smaller male cocoons in outermost cells. From top to bottom, the numbers of female cocoons are four, three, and two, respectively.

The fifth-stage larva inside the cocoon is called a prepupa (Figure 10), and undergoes a summer dormant period that may last one or two months, depending on local temperatures and the geographic origin of the population. As explained in section 4.2, the prepupal stage lasts longer in populations from warmer areas. By late summer, the prepupa molts into a white pupa (Figure 10). A few days later, the eyes of the pupa, and then other parts of the body, begin to darken, until they become completely black (Figure 10). At this point, the pupa looks similar to an adult, but its wings are not fully developed and its entire body is still covered by the shiny translucent pupal skin. After approximately one month, the pupa molts into an adult and remains dormant inside the cocoon until the next spring (Figure 11). Newly formed adults are soft and their hairs appear wet. Older adults have a hardened cuticle and dry hairs.

Figure 10. Left to right: blue orchard bee prepupa, white pupa (side view), and black pupa (ventral view) in cut cocoons.

Figure 11. Male blue orchard bee adult in cut cocoon (ventral view).

During the winter dormant period (Figure 6), BOBs need to be exposed to cold temperatures to successfully over-winter and emerge the following spring. This cold exposure can occur under natural winter conditions or in a refrigerator (e.g., at 39–41°F [3–5°C]). The duration of this dormant period depends on the local climatic conditions of each zone and the origin of the population. As explained in section 4.2, BOBs from higher latitudes require longer wintering periods than those from lower latitudes.

Emergence commences as temperatures rise in the spring. The bees chew their way out of the cocoon and break through mud partitions and nest debris to emerge from the nest. If a bee has died, those located deeper in the nest simply chew through the dead body. Emergence is timed so that males (located in the outermost cells) emerge one to three days before females. Once out of the nest, newly emerged adults excrete their meconium as a few drops of whitish, quickly solidifying secretion evacuated from the anus. The meconium contains metabolic waste products. Adults then engage immediately in mating activities or fly to nearby flowers to take nectar.

2.3. Foraging Behavior and Pollinating Efficacy

BOBs collect pollen and nectar from a wide array of wild plants (Figure 12), but they show a strong preference for fruit tree flowers when they are available. Pollen samples from BOB nests built in or near orchards typically contain 85 to 100 percent fruit tree pollen. This preference ensures that BOBs will not wander onto other plants and ignore the target crop. Known pollen sources from both wild and managed populations are listed in Table 1. Other flower-visiting records (though not necessarily involving pollen collection) are listed in Appendix 1, page 74.

At fruit tree flowers, female BOBs collect nectar and pollen simultaneously. They take nectar from the base of the corolla with their tongue (proboscis), while they vigorously scrabble the an-

Figure 12. Male blue orchard bee on dandelion. Dandelions and other early-blooming plants provide temporary floral resources for blue orchard bees emerging before orchard bloom.

Table 1. Pollens found in blue orchard bee provisions.

PLANT FAMILY	SCIENTIFIC NAME	COMMON NAMES	COMMENTS
Asteraceae	*Taraxacum officinale*	Dandelion	
Berberidaceae	*Berberis repens* [=*Mahonia repens*]	Creeping Oregon grape	
Brassicaceae	*Brassica napus*	Turnip	In confinement
	Brassica rapa	Rape; Canola	In confinement
	Sinapis alba	White mustard	In confinement
Ericaceae	*Arctostaphylos* sp.	Manzanita; Bearberry; Arctostaphylos	
Fabaceae	*Lathyrus* sp.	Sweet pea	
	Cercis occidentalis	Western redbud	
Grossulariaceae	*Ribes* sp.	Currant, Gooseberry	
Hydrophyllaceae	*Hydrophyllum capitatum*	Ballhead Waterleaf; Cat's breeches	Dominant in wild habitats
	Phacelia hastata	Silverleaf Phacelia; Silverleaf Scorpionweed	Dominant in wild habitats
	Phacelia humilis	Low Phacelia; Low Scorpionweed	
	Phacelia tanacetifolia	Lacy Phacelia; Lacy Scorpionweed	
Limnanthaceae	*Limnanthes alba*	White Meadowfoam	Dominant in meadowfoam fields
Liliaceae	*Camassia quamash*	Common Camas; Small Camas	
Ranunculaceae	*Delphinium nuttallianum*	Low Larkspur; Two-lobe Larkspur	
	Ranunculus sp.	Buttercup	
Rhamnaceae	*Ceanothus* sp.	Ceanothus; Buckbrush; California Lilac	
Rosaceae	*Malus domestica*	Apple	Dominant in orchards
	Potentilla sp.	Cinquefoil; Potentilla	
	Prunus spp.	Almond, Plum, Prune, Cherry, Peach, Nectarine	Dominant in orchards
	Purshia tridentata	Bitterbrush	Dominant in wild habitats
	Pyrus communis	Pear	Dominant in orchards
Salicaceae	*Salix lasiolepis*	Arroyo Willow	Dominant in wild habitats
	Salix lemmonii	Lemmon's Willow	Dominant in wild habitats

thers using their scopa, as well as their middle and hind legs. This behavior ensures thorough contact with the stigmas and the anthers of the flower on virtually every visit (Figure 13). Males only take nectar, but because they always land on the reproductive organs of the flower, they also provide valuable pollination services (Figure 14). Both male and female BOBs readily move from tree to tree and row to row. Thus, BOBs facilitate cross-pollination, rather than pollination within a tree or within a cultivar. This behavior is particularly important for pollination of self-incompatible fruit trees.

As early spring bees, BOBs are better adapted for flying under poor weather conditions than most other bees. BOBs forage and pollinate under overcast skies and at temperatures as low as 54°F (12°C), when other bees are barely active. During good weather, BOBs also begin foraging earlier in the morning and end later in the afternoon.

These behavioral traits make the BOB a very desirable fruit tree pollinator. As few as 250 nesting females per acre (625 per ha) are enough to maximize pollination on apples, and 300 nesting females per acre (740 per ha) enough to pollinate almonds! These estimates are very close to those calculated for the hornfaced bee, *Osmia corni-*

Figure 13. A blue orchard bee female pollinates an apple flower. Note positioning of the body on the reproductive organs of the flower.

Figure 14. Blue orchard bee male on cherry flower. As with females, positioning of the body on the reproductive organs of the flower ensures pollination.

frons, in Japan (200 to 240 nesting females per acre of apples) and the horned bee, *Osmia cornuta,* in Spain (215 females per acre of apples, 300 females per acre of almonds). By contrast, 1 to 2.5 strong honey bee hives per acre (two to six hives per ha), with thousands of foragers in each, are recommended to pollinate the same crops. The need for greater numbers of honey bees is explained by their tendency to visit other plants, their less frequent stigma contact during fruit tree flower visits, and their inability to fly under marginal weather conditions.

A three-year study in northern Utah demonstrated that yields in a commercial cherry orchard were dramatically increased when BOBs were used as pollinators (Table 2). In 1992 and 1997, freezing temperatures killed most flowers in the orchard. In 1999, with freezing temperatures killing 46 percent of the flowers in the orchard, and particularly bad weather conditions during the remainder of the blooming period, the yield obtained was comparable to yields obtained in years with good weather with honey bees (Table 2). Most local growers did not obtain harvestable yields in 1999. Record yields in 1998 and 2000 were accompanied by high BOB returns.

Table 2. Cherry yields and female blue orchard bee (BOB) returns in a cherry orchard in North Ogden, Utah.

YEAR	POLLINATOR	CHERRY YIELDS (in pounds)	FEMALE BOB POPULATION INCREASE
1992	Honey bee	No harvest	–
1993	Honey bee	6,700	–
1994	Honey bee	12,225	–
1995	Honey bee	10,625	–
1996	Honey bee	8,150	–
1997	Honey bee	No harvest	–
1998	BOB	32,800	5.4-fold
1999	BOB	9,155	2.1-fold
2000	BOB	37,335	4.2-fold

3
ARTIFICIAL NESTING MATERIALS

BOBs accept a wide variety of man-made nesting materials. A continuously updated list of companies providing nesting materials for BOBs is available at the Logan Bee Biology and Systematics Laboratory web site (http://www.LoganBeeLab.usu.edu). Various nesting materials differ in their affordability, manageability, durability, attractiveness to BOB females, and accessibility to parasites. Regardless of the type of nesting material used, the dimensions of the nesting cavities themselves are extremely important for obtaining healthy BOB populations.

3.1. Types of Nesting Materials

Several nesting unit designs have been tested for BOBs. Most of them conform, with some variations, to one of four types: solid blocks, hollow boxes, grooved boards, and reeds. BOB females accept nesting materials of different colors, but are somewhat less attracted to white surfaces.

Solid blocks. A solid wood block with drilled holes (Figure 15) is the artificial nesting unit most similar to abandoned beetle burrows in a dead tree typically used by wild BOBs. Drilling across — rather than with — the wood grain results in cavities with smoother inside walls, which facilitates insertion of paper straws (see below). Holes can be drilled all the way to the back of the block, in which case some backing material (e.g., wood board) should be used to close the bottom of the cavity. Any crevices should be sealed to prevent entry of both light and small parasites. Adhesive aluminum foil can be used as a backing material, but it is necessary to dust the cavities with sand to reduce reflectiveness and cover the exposed adhesive surface at the end of the cavity. Alternatively, slightly shorter holes may be drilled so that no backing material is necessary. It is important to waterproof wood blocks, even inside the nest cavities, in advance, and to let them dry before use. The vapors of many wood finishing materials repel BOB females and may cause mortality in early immature stages. However, without waterproofing, materials tend to swell with increasing humidity, causing cavities to shrink.

Figure 15. Wood block with inserted paper straws.

BOB females nest readily in well-insulated drilled wood blocks. However, it is highly advisable to insert paraffin-coated paper straws into the cavities, allowing for easy retrieval and inspection of the nests. Some commercially available paper straws are semi-translucent and allow for easy inspection of nest contents when held against a light source. Non-paraffined straws sometimes wick humidity from the pollen-nectar provisions and increase larval mortality. Plastic straws and paper straws coated with plastic-like materials are not suitable either, as they tend to promote condensation within the cells and high immature mortality. When using wood blocks that are not drilled all the way through the back of the block, it is advisable to seal the inserted end of paper straws. Otherwise, the inner-most cocoon may remain attached to the bottom of the nesting cavity when the straw is pulled out of the block. The bottom of paper straws can be sealed with paraffin, wax, hot glue, etc. Paper straws should be flush with the nesting cavity entrance to facilitate bee movements on the surface of the nesting block. BOB females prefer to nest in straws with the entrance orifice painted a flat black, rather than in completely white straws.

Paper straws can be inserted in thick cardboard tubes. These provide extra protection against parasites that otherwise could oviposit through the thin paper straw (see section 8.1). Cardboard tubes can be used without paper liners, but they are harder to dissect and inspect than paper straws. For a more affordable, lighter type of nesting unit, styrene, rather than wood, blocks can be used with acceptable results. However, during particularly warm days, in-nest temperatures may become too warm in styrene solid blocks.

Hollow boxes. Several types of hollow nesting units, which are light and easy to manage, are shown in Figures 16 to 18. Milk cartons (Figure 16) consist of a front wood board with drilled holes, through which paper straws sealed at the back are inserted, encased in a milk

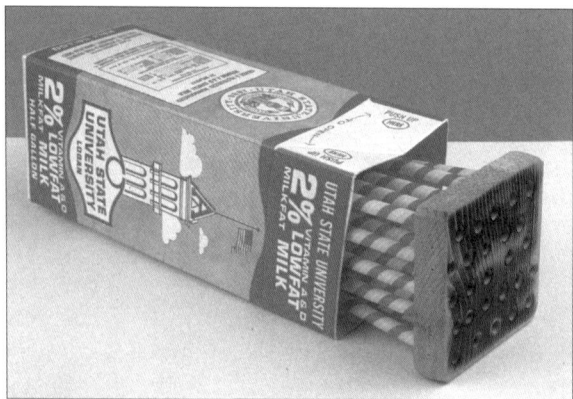

Figure 16. Milk carton nesting unit with front board pulled out to show paper straws.

Figure 17. Paraffin-coated cardboard box with cardboard tubes and inserted paper straws.

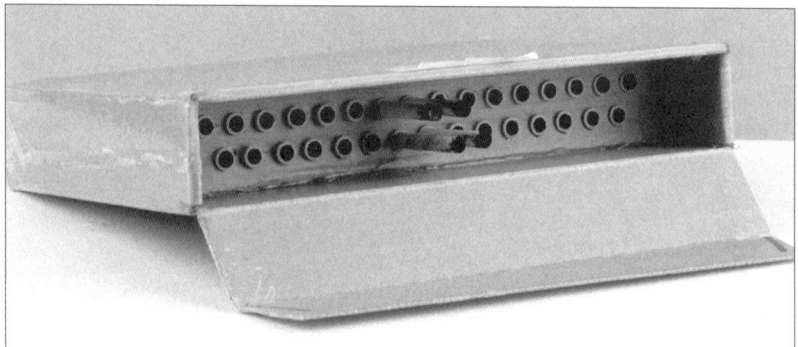

container. As with solid blocks, paper straws can be inserted in cardboard tubes. Similar nesting materials can be built using paraffin-coated cardboard (Figure 17), wood (Figure 18), or some other waterproof material that does not trap excess moisture. Again, it is important to seal any cracks or openings that might allow the entrance of light and parasites into the nesting unit.

Grooved boards. Grooved boards, or wafer boards, are shown in Figure 19. They can be stacked to attain the desired number of holes per nesting unit and be easily disassembled for nest inspection. Grooved boards should be tightly clasped together to prevent crevices through which light, parasites, and water might access the nesting cavity. They can be used with or without paper or card-

Figure 18. Wooden box with cardboard tubes and inserted paper straws.

Figure 19. Grooved boards and assembled grooved board nesting unit.

board inserts. When used without inserts, female BOBs tend to seal the joint between wafers along the nesting cavity with mud.

Reeds. Reeds from *Phragmites* and bamboo also can be used as nesting materials for BOBs (Figure 20). They are lightweight and easy to obtain. Reed sections should be cut so that the front of the nesting cavity is open and the back is sealed by the reed node. The back of the reed may be painted or made opaque if necessary. Reeds can be easily split length-wise for nest inspection. A reed nest should be split by holding the reed section tightly in one hand and applying a knife blade at the node to pry the halves of the reed open.

Figure 20. Reed bundle in milk carton attached to pear tree trunk.

For commercial-scale management, only nesting materials that allow for easy manipulation of nests (transport, inspection, etc.) should be considered. For example, wood blocks with nest cavities without paper inserts can be used to encourage BOB nesting at a given site, but they are not truly manageable. It is also important to note that simple bundles of paper straws yield extremely poor results, as these nesting units do not provide enough protection against light and parasitism and are insufficiently attractive to BOB females.

3.2. Cavity Dimensions

Optimal cavity dimensions for BOBs are 19/64 inches (7.5 mm) in diameter and 6 inches (15 cm) long. Nests built in shorter or narrower (even 0.5 mm narrower) cavities typically contain fewer cells and small-sized, highly male-biased progeny. Cavities wider than 19/64 inches (7.5 mm) or longer than 6 inches (15 cm) may contain more cells and/or more female progeny, but they are somewhat less attractive to bees and more difficult to drill and manage. When using inserts (paper straws by themselves or inserted in cardboard tubes), cavities wider than 19/64 inches (7.5 mm), need to be drilled to accommodate for the extra thickness of the insert walls. Cavity width should be arranged so that inserts are easy to pull with a pair of forceps, but will not fall off when the nesting unit is inverted. Controlling for exact diameters and lengths is difficult when reeds are used. In this case, inside diameters ranging from 0.26–0.33 inches (6.5–8.5 mm) and lengths of 6 inches (15 cm) or more should be selected.

Nesting BOB females prefer a space surrounding each nest cavity. Adequate spacing between cavities helps reduce confusion and wasted "search time" by nesting females. Inter-cavity spaces also are used by females as landing platforms and basking perches. In solid blocks, hollow boxes, and grooved boards, distances between holes (from center to center) should be about 0.75 inches (2 cm) (Figures 15–19). Nesting units with closer holes tend to be less attractive to BOB females. In reed nesting units (Figure 20), distance between entrances can be increased by using sections of different lengths. The three-dimensional pattern provided in this way helps females locate their nest cavities. The distance from the outermost nest cavities to the outer edges of wood blocks and grooved boards should be at least 0.75 inches (2 cm) to avoid parasitism by the chalcid wasp *Leucospis affinis* (see section 8.3).

4
HOW TO REAR BOB POPULATIONS

The life cycle of the BOB can be divided into five overlapping periods (Figure 6, page 9): *nesting period*, during which adult females build nests and lay eggs; *developmental period*, during which progeny develop from eggs to adults; *pre-wintering period*, during which adults inside their cocoons are exposed to warm temperatures prior to wintering; *wintering period*, during which adults inside their cocoons are exposed to cool temperatures; and *incubation-emergence period*, during which wintered adults are exposed to warm temperatures that stimulate emergence and subsequent mating.

A general account of adequate conditions for BOB nesting is given below, followed by instructions on how to handle nests during development, pre-wintering, and wintering periods. Two possible scenarios are provided: rearing local populations under near-natural conditions, and rearing populations under artificial conditions. Finally, information is given on how to incubate populations and predict emergence. More detailed information on how to release large populations in commercial orchards is provided in section 5. An approximate calendar of the main activities involved in BOB management is shown in Figure 6 (page 9).

4.1. Nesting

When nesting units are placed in the field, either in orchard-garden environments or in natural nesting sites, they need protection from rain and wind and, in warm areas, from direct sunlight. Nesting units should be set up so cavities are horizontal or with entrances tilted down slightly to prevent rainwater from entering. Nesting materials should be placed in the field before nesting begins (Figure 6, page 9). Because female cells are mostly formed at the beginning of the nesting period, materials placed too late in the nesting period will yield nests with mostly male progeny. Nesting materials should be securely fastened to prevent any kind of movement that could dislodge eggs and young larvae from pollen-nectar provisions.

Nesting units can be placed individually, attached (tied or nailed) to trees, posts, or fences (Figure 20, page 20). Alternatively, materials can be grouped in nesting shelters such as those in Figures 21 and 22. BOB females will readily nest in both kinds of situations. Large visual landmarks such as buildings, fences, or the nesting shelter itself ap-

Figure 21. One of many types of nesting shelters: wood box attached to a cherry tree. Note chicken wire to prevent bird and mouse damage.

How to Rear BOB Populations / 23

Figure 22. Another type of nesting shelter: weather shelter on metal fence posts.

pear to help females locate their nesting site. Nesting materials should be placed three to five feet (1–1.5 m) above the ground or higher.

In addition to adequate nesting cavities and pollen-nectar resources (Table 1, page 13), BOB females require a mud source to build cell partitions. Irrigation ditches or leaking irrigation pipes frequently provide adequate mud sources. If these are not available, a shallow trench may be dug near the nesting site and kept moist during the nesting period. Managed mud sources can be covered with a coarse grid (1.5 inches [37 mm]) screen to prevent bird predation of BOB females during mud collection (Figure 23). Installing nesting units near mud and flower sources will shorten foraging trips and increase cell production rate and pollination.

Figure 23. Mud source protected with chicken wire screen to avoid bird predation.

Once nesting activities have started, nesting materials should not be relocated or otherwise manipulated. Nesting females become disoriented even when their nesting cavity is moved only a few inches away, and usually abscond if their nesting site is severely disturbed. Nesting populations should be moved only under special circumstances and with necessary precautions outlined in sections 6.2 and 7.2. Nesting units oriented to the south, east, or southeast allow for more hours of foraging activity and are most attractive to nesting females. Under favorable conditions, average production rates of one cell per day per female can be expected.

The nesting period of a managed BOB population typically lasts more than a month (Figure 6, page 9). However, individual females are rarely active for that long. Toward the end of their adult lives, females have tattered wings, lose hair, and move more slowly. They produce fewer and smaller cells compared to young bees, and lay mostly male eggs. Old females sometimes plug empty cavities around their last provisioned nest. These plugs are very thin and break easily. Toward the end of the nesting period, BOB parasites and predators are more abundant. For these reasons, it is advisable to remove nesting materials from the field before nesting completely ends. Nesting materials can be removed when only visibly aged females and few or no males are seen at the nesting site. This will be accompanied by a dramatic decline in flight activity (sometimes despite good weather and adequate food resources) and a decrease in the number of completed nests (plugged entrances) per day.

Nesting materials removed from the orchard should be taken to a storage area where they can be kept throughout the remainder of the growing season (Figure 6, page 9). Recently built nests contain individuals in the egg and early larval stages that if jostled can be dislodged from the provisions. When this happens, the young larva is usually unable to reattach to the provision and starves. For this reason, nesting units need to be handled carefully. A good way to transport and store nesting materials is with the nest entrances facing up, so potentially dislodged immatures will still remain in contact with their pollen-nectar provision.

4.2. Development, Pre-wintering, and Wintering

The conditions (mainly temperature) to which BOBs are exposed during development, pre-wintering, and wintering are extremely important, as they not only affect survival, but also vigor, time of emergence, establishment, and ultimate nesting and pollinating performance. We discuss two different scenarios. In the first one, BOBs are reared locally under natural or close-to-natural conditions. In the second scenario, BOBs are reared under artificial conditions.

Local populations under natural conditions. BOBs from local populations and stored under near-natural conditions during the spring, summer, and winter are easier to rear. After the nesting period is over, nesting materials should be placed in a shady area, such as a barn, a garage, or a porch. Open or ventilated areas work better, as they are less likely to overheat and accumulate excessive moisture. Direct sunlight or locations prone to flooding should be avoided. During this period, some larvae spin their cocoons in a reversed position (with the nipple toward the nest bottom). When those bees attempt to emerge, they move toward the inner portion of the nest and ultimately die within the nest, possibly killing other bees in the process. This problem is solved by keeping the nesting materials with the cavity entrances facing up during development, as larvae use gravity as a cue to spin their cocoons pointing toward the nest entrance. Paper straws or cardboard tubes may be left in the nesting materials throughout the development period. Alternatively, inserts may be pulled out of the nesting units. This should be done preferably after cocoon spinning to avoid damaging eggs and larvae. Nests in paper straws, cardboard tubes, or reeds are better stored in shallow, ventilated containers. Trapped humidity causes pollen to mold and slows BOB development. For the same reason, BOB nests should not be stacked more than three layers high. Precautions to protect nests from mice, predatory ants, and parasitic wasps during the spring and summer are explained in section 8.

Developmental rates for BOBs nesting from April to May and kept in a north-facing open barn in North Logan, Utah, are shown in Figure 24 (orchard regime). It is very important to monitor development and establish an approximate calendar of key developmental events (cocoon spinning, pupation, adulthood) under local conditions. Such a calendar can be used in future years as a guideline to determine appropriate wintering dates, emergence periods, etc., as illustrated in Figure 6 (page 9). For most of the development, checks should be

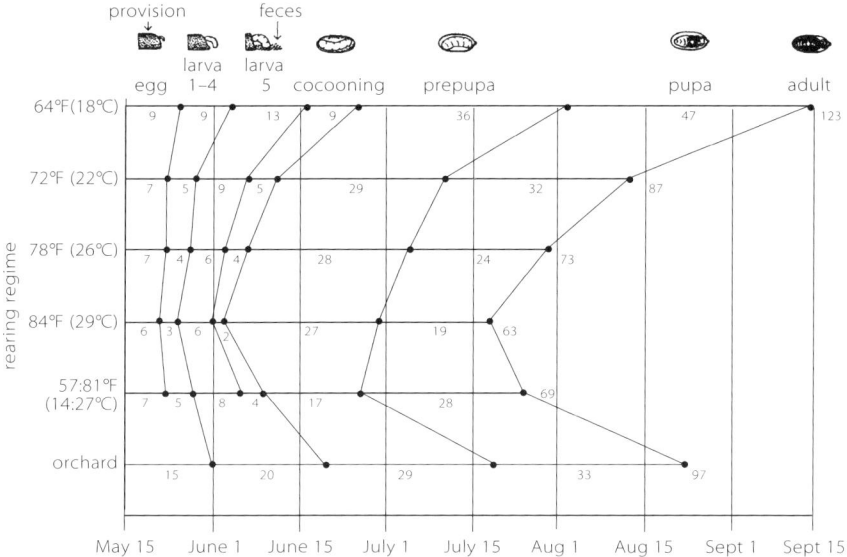

Figure 24. Duration of developmental stages of blue orchard bees from northern Utah at various temperature treatments. Recently built cells were exposed to five artificial temperature regimes (constant 64, 72, 78 and 84°F, and fluctuating 57:81°F [8 hours at 57°F and 16 hours at 81°F]), and to natural conditions (nests kept in a north-facing barn in an apple orchard) in North Logan, Utah. Numbers below the lines indicate average duration of each developmental stage. Numbers to the right of each line indicate average development time from egg to adult. At 64°F, 17 percent of the bees remained in the prepupal stage.

conducted once a month or so. Then, as bees reach adulthood, more frequent monitoring is needed (Figure 6, page 9). An easy way to check for developmental stages is to randomly select some cocoons and cut them open around the nipple area with a razor blade. Because different individuals within a population may be at different developmental stages, about 10 cocoons taken from several different nests should be checked every time. Immature bees in open cocoons are exposed to increased desiccation and are likely to die. To avoid sacrificing females, which do most of the pollination, small cocoons in the outermost cells of the nest should be inspected. A less intrusive way to check for developmental stages is to X-ray nests (Figure 25). On me-

Figure 25. X-ray plate of blue orchard bee nests containing adults. Nest entrances are to the right.

dium-grain industrial film, exposure times of 30 seconds at voltages of 25 KV provide good images of nests in paper straws, cardboard tubes, and reeds. These voltages, which are not harmful to bees, can be obtained with industrial and mammography X-ray machines.

Once the first adult bees are detected, developmental checks should be done once a week, with about 20 male cocoons inspected per bee population or stock. At that time, it is important to check some female cocoons as well, because average female development may follow average male development by a few days. In local populations reared under near-natural conditions, bees should reach adulthood in synchrony with the decline of ambient temperatures. Then, nests can be left in unheated storage areas throughout the winter (Figure 6, page 9). Emergence is expected to coincide with the emergence of local populations the following spring. If summer temperatures in the storage area are significantly warmer than ambient temperatures, managed BOB populations may reach adulthood before late summer or autumn temperatures drop. Then, nests need to be wintered artificially to avoid prolonged exposure of pre-wintering adults to warm temperatures.

Artificial conditions. Manipulating emergence periods is best achieved under artificial temperature regimes. This is important when pollinating a crop whose flowering period does not coincide with the natural emergence period of the bee population. Artificial conditions also are recommended when the BOB population comes from a geographical area with a climate different from the rearing area. An extreme case of this situation, involving the use of late-flying (April to May) populations from northern Utah to pollinate early-flowering almonds in California, is described in section 5.4. All recommendations made for rearing under natural conditions (such as keeping nesting materials upward until cocoon spinning, avoiding excessive humidity, monitoring development, and preventing parasitism and predation) also apply to populations reared artificially.

Rearing under artificial conditions requires incubation and wintering units with controlled temperatures. Relative humidity in the incubation units should be maintained around 70 percent during development.

BOBs from northern Utah, which fly in April and May, should not be reared at constant temperatures below 72°F (22°C). At lower temperatures, bees develop slowly and some fail to reach adulthood, remaining in the prepupal stage throughout the summer, fall, and win-

Table 3. Developmental and winter mortality in blue orchard bees from northern Utah reared in the laboratory at different temperatures, and in an open north-facing barn in an apple orchard in North Logan, Utah. All bees were wintered at 39°F (4°C) for 215 days. Developmental mortality percentages are somewhat high, in part due to necessary manipulation during the study.

REARING TEMPERATURE	% DEVELOPMENTAL MORTALITY	% WINTER MORTALITY
64°F (18°C)	42	26
72°F (22°C)	19	11
79°F (26°C)	13	4
84°F (29°C)	16	5
57:81°F (14:27°C)	11	2
Orchard	12	6

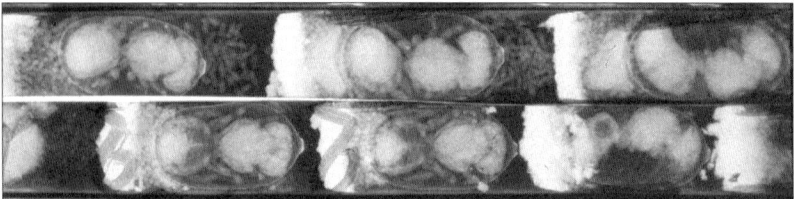

Figure 26. X-ray plate showing adult blue orchard bees with white (full) (top row) and partially black (empty) (bottom row) abdomens. White abdomens indicate the presence of well developed fat bodies. Black abdomens indicate partial fat body depletion and decreased bee vigor.

ter (Figure 24, Table 3). These bees do not develop into healthy adults. At higher temperatures (up to 84°F [29°C]), bees develop faster because the larval and pupal stages are shortened (Figure 24), while maintaining acceptable survival (Table 3). At fluctuating temperatures (daily cycle of eight hours at 57°F [14°C] and 16 hours at 81°F [27°C]; average daily temperature: 72°F [22°C]), BOBs also develop faster (Figure 24) and have good survival (Table 3). In this case, however, the faster development results from a shortened prepupal period (Figure 24). BOB populations from lower latitudes (e.g. central Texas), which fly in February to March, develop more slowly because they have longer prepupal periods and require temperatures of at least 75°F (24°C) to develop. At 72°F (22°C), some individuals from these early-flying populations fail to reach adulthood.

Adult BOBs within their cocoons maintain high metabolic rates unless they are chilled. Pre-wintering adults kept for too long at warm temperatures use up their metabolic reserves and are likely to die during the winter — or emerge as weak, non-viable individuals the following spring. X-ray images of these individuals are recognizable by their partially black (empty) abdomens, in contrast to healthy individuals whose abdomens appear white (filled with well-developed fat bodies) (Figure 26). In wild and managed populations reared locally under natural conditions, fat body depletion is not a major concern, as bees reach adulthood in synchrony with natural declines in ambient temperatures. However, populations reared under artificial conditions require appropriate developmental monitoring and management of pre-wintering periods. Populations from different geographical areas or exposed to different rearing conditions will develop at different rates, so development checks should be performed separate for each population or bee "lot."

Ideally, to avoid excessive fat body depletion, BOBs should be cooled two to four weeks after adulthood. Because not all individuals in a population reach adulthood at the same time, managed populations can be cooled one to three weeks after 100 percent of the sampled cocoons contain adults. Pre-wintering periods also should be carefully managed when BOBs are reared under near-natural conditions in a barn or garage that is significantly warmer than ambient temperatures, or when bees from high latitudes or altitudes are reared under near-natural conditions in a warmer geographical area. Under such circumstances, BOBs tend to complete development before ambient temperatures start to decline. Populations should then be cooled as indicated above. Artificial cooling can be achieved by moving populations to a refrigerator or a walk-in cooler. Gradual cooling regimes, with one or two intermediate steps, work better than transferring bees directly from hot to cold temperatures.

Both wintering duration and temperature influence bee survival and emergence timing. BOBs from northern Utah winter well at 39°F (4°C) for 180 to 200 days. Bees cooled in September or October are ready to emerge by April or May of the following year. Wintering periods can be prolonged by a month without serious consequences for bee survival. Wintering periods shorter than 150 days do not increase bee mortality, but they excessively extend emergence periods (Figure 27), making synchronization between BOB nesting and blooming of the target crop difficult to accomplish (see section 4.3). When wintered at warmer temperatures, BOBs emerge faster. For example, BOBs from northern Utah wintered for 150 days emerge faster when wintered at 45°F (7°C) compared to 39°F (4°C) (Figure 27). However, if kept at 45°F (7°C) for more than 150 days, these bees will start emerging in the cooler. At 50°F (10°C) emergence within the cooler will start even earlier. At lower temperatures (e.g., 32°F [0°C]), BOBs from northern Utah have high survival, but take longer to emerge (see Figure 27 and section 4.3). Early-flying populations from lower latitudes

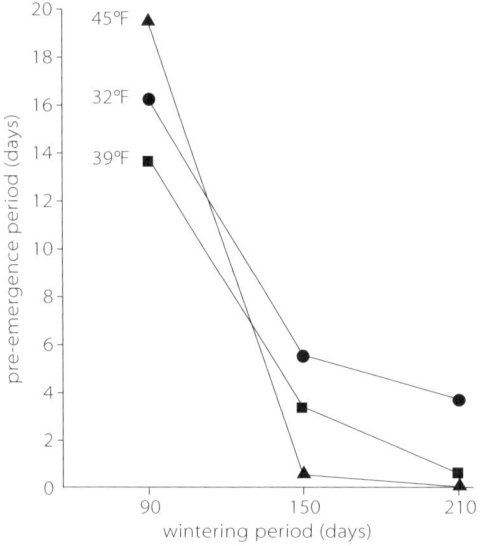

Figure 27. Mean male pre-emergence periods (days from incubation at 68°F [20°C] to emergence) in BOBs from northern Utah wintered at 32°F (0°C), 39°F (4°C), and 45°F (7°C) for 90, 150, and 210 days. At 45°F, many males emerged in the cooler when wintered for more than 150 days.

or altitudes are naturally exposed to shorter, warmer winters. Accordingly, these populations require shorter wintering periods and tolerate warmer wintering temperatures. As mentioned, these populations also reach adulthood later.

4.3. Incubation and Emergence

Learning to predict and manipulate bee emergence is very important to synchronize peak nesting period with peak bloom of the target crop. If bees have been exposed to an adequate wintering period, male emergence should start on the first day of incubation, and female emergence should follow by one to three days. Emergence of 80 to 100 percent of the population should be completed in about a week.

Populations reared and wintered in barns or unheated garages should emerge more or less in synchrony with local wild BOB populations. One or two weeks before expected bloom, nests with bees can be inserted into nesting units set up at the orchard or garden that needs to be pollinated. As the weather warms, bees will start emerging. In populations wintered under artificial conditions, emergence periods can be programmed ahead of time by manipulating the duration of the wintering period and/or the wintering temperature (see

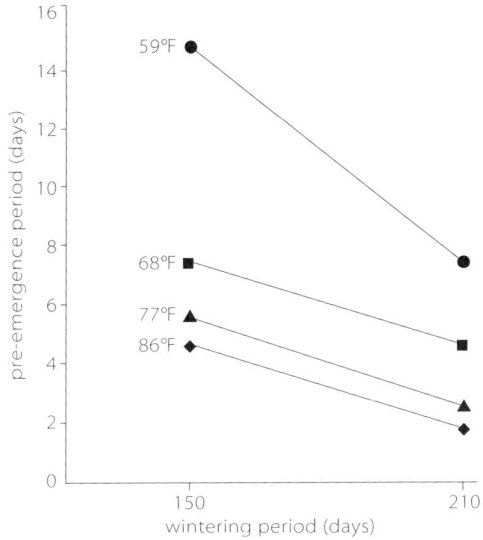

Figure 28. Mean female pre-emergence periods (days from incubation to emergence) in BOBs from northern Utah wintered at 39°F (4°C) for 150 and 210 days, and incubated at 59°F (15°C), 68°F (20°C), 77°F (25°C), and 86°F (30°C). Some bees failed to emerge at 86°F (30°C).

Figure 27 and section 4.2). Bees wintered for longer periods and/or at milder temperatures will emerge sooner and faster than bees exposed to brief and/or cold wintering.

Sometimes, if males start to emerge in the winter storage area before the expected bloom of the target crop, it may be necessary to delay bee emergence. In this case, nests can be transferred to a refrigerator at 37–41°F (3–5°C) to delay emergence. BOBs usually can be held at these temperatures at least an additional month, although extending chilling more than two months will affect bee vigor and survival.

If emergence needs to be advanced to improve timing with bloom, nests can be incubated artificially. Best results (prompt and fast emergence) are obtained when BOBs are incubated at temperatures no lower than 68°F (20°C). At a constant 59°F (15°C), BOB females take too long to emerge for precise timing with orchard bloom, even when wintered for long (210 days) periods (Figure 28). At 86°F (30°C), emergence is shortened compared to 68–77°F (20–25°C) (Figure 28) but mortality is slightly increased.

To gauge how soon a BOB population may emerge, a sample of male cocoons should be taken out of the wintering area about two weeks before expected bloom and exposed to room temperature (around 72°F [22°C]). If males do not start emerging after 24 to 48 hours of incubation, the population probably needs artificial incubation to speed up emergence. Methods to artificially incubate populations are described in section 5.1.

5

HOW TO RELEASE BOB POPULATIONS IN ORCHARDS

During the months before bloom, several important decisions need to be made concerning when and how to release BOB populations. In this section, we explain how to time bee emergence with bloom and discuss release methods, optimum population sizes, and the number of nesting cavities and their distribution within the orchard. All of these factors affect both bee reproduction and pollination.

5.1. Timing BOB Emergence with Orchard Bloom

In garden situations, with few flowers to pollinate and several plant species blooming consecutively, precise timing of BOB emergence with bloom of a particular plant is generally not a major concern. In commercial orchards, however, timing is critical. If females emerge when there are still no open flowers, many will disperse to search for blooming plants and nest elsewhere. If bees are released too late, the valuable early bloom will not be pollinated. Because most commercial orchards only bloom for two to three weeks, bees may not have enough pollen-nectar resources for adequate nesting if they miss too many days of bloom. From a fruit production perspective, although not all the flowers need to be pollinated for maximum fruit set, pollination of early flowers normally ensures better yields and/or larger fruits (see section 1). Another important reason for pollinating early flowers is that inclement weather may seriously limit the number of days conducive to bee activity during the remainder of the flowering period. Alternative flower sources — such as dandelion, willows, and fruit trees of early-flowering cultivars or species — are important nectar sources for bees that emerge before bloom initiation of the target crop (Figure 12, page 12). Ideally, females should begin to emerge and mate with the first bloom of the target crop. In this way, after a one- to two-day pre-nesting period, most females start nesting before peak bloom occurs.

To decide when to release a BOB population, it is important to monitor flower bud development and weather forecasts. This will provide an idea of when to expect first bloom. As explained above, incubation of some male cocoons at room temperature is a good way to predict how fast the BOB population will emerge. If a population is ready to emerge (males emerge in 24 to 48 hours when incubated at room temperature) and daily temperatures in the week following release are expected to be in the 70s°F (21–27°C), nests with unemerged bees can be installed at the nesting sites, without further incubation, approximately a week before expected first bloom. If daily temperatures are expected to be in the mid-50s or 60s°F (13–20°C), populations should be further incubated, because BOB emergence progresses slowly at those temperatures (Figure 28), despite the continuation of fruit tree flower development.

BOB nests can be incubated at 72 to 85°F (22–29°C) in an incubation box, such as the one shown in Figure 29. An incubation box is an opaque container with an opening through which bees can exit. Emerging males, which exit before females, are attracted to an adjacent light source and collected in an attached transparent container. To avoid exposing emerged bees to warm temperatures for too long, the attached container should be checked no less frequently than daily, and taken to a refrigerator (37–41°F [3–5°C]) when a significant number of males has accumulated. The first females start appearing when approximately half of the males have emerged. At this point, the entire population (including the emerged bees kept in the refrigerator) can be released in the orchard — or cooled if bloom has not begun. This method allows for very precise timing of female emergence with bloom initiation.

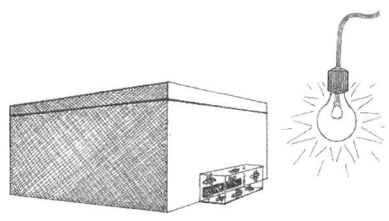

Figure 29. Incubation box. Note slit at the base of right side, and light to attract emerging bees to the attached transparent container.

A second possibility is to incubate BOB populations within the release shelter. Shelter designs creating warmer conditions than ambient and promoting BOB emergence are currently under study. As mentioned, once BOBs have emerged and established, they fly and pollinate flowers at temperatures as low as 54°F (12°C).

5.2. Release Methods

It is best to place BOB populations in the orchard in the evening or early morning, and on days with fair weather. Rain and wind encourage pre-nesting female dispersal. Because it is sometimes difficult to accurately predict spring weather, populations can be split in two or three groups to be released on different days. This staggered release method also increases the chances of good timing with bloom initiation, and females of the later groups will be attracted to nesting sites by females of the groups preceding them.

As a rule, BOB populations should be set out within their natal nests. Females that chew their way out of the nest through mud partitions and remnants of sibling cocoons have lower pre-nesting dispersal than bees emerged from loose cocoons. Under favorable conditions, such as good weather at release time, sufficient pollen-nectar resources, and following adequate rearing and wintering regimes, dispersal in populations released from natal nests should be no higher than 20 percent. Occasionally, populations have to be released as loose cocoons, in a method called mass release, because of heavy chalkbrood or hairy-fingered mite infestations (see sections 8.12 and 8.13). In populations released as loose cocoons, high pre-nesting female dispersal (up to 50 percent) can be expected. If it is necessary to work with loose cocoons, female cocoons may be inserted individually into the bottoms of the nesting cavities. If this is too time-consuming, cocoons should, at least, be placed in some kind of emergence box, such as a wooden or cardboard box with holes through which bees can fly.

Normally, BOB females prefer to nest in new cavities rather than in old, used ones. Pre-used cavities contain debris that females must remove or push to the back of the nest. Pre-used cavities also may harbor diseases and parasites. Because female BOBs may build one to seven nests throughout their life span, three to five new nesting cavities should be provided per female expected to emerge and establish.

Nesting materials can be concentrated in one or a few nesting shelters, or evenly distributed across the orchard. Although concentrating all nesting materials in a large nesting shelter may be more convenient, female establishment tends to be better when nesting materials are distributed in smaller groups. Whichever method is used, it is important that bees are released at all nesting shelters. Although females will drift from shelter to shelter, many will nest at the shelter from which they emerged. Shelters containing only empty nesting cavities tend to have poor establishment. Once a female builds her first nest at a shelter, she will tend to continue nesting at that shelter for as long as nesting cavities and floral and mud resources are available.

Distribution of nesting shelters evenly across the orchard also provides more uniform pollination. This will be especially noticeable in years with poor weather and few periods of acceptable flight conditions for bees. In the presence of abundant bloom, BOB females tend to forage within 300 feet (100 m) of their nesting sites. Thus, to avoid excessive overlap between the foraging areas of bees nesting in different shelters, distance between nesting shelters should, ideally, be about 300 feet (100 m). For the same reason, if all bees are released at one shelter, this should be placed in the center of the orchard.

5.3. Bees per Acre

The number of BOBs necessary to provide optimum pollination for an acre of orchard depends on many factors, including the fruit tree species or cultivar, and the ratio and distribution of pollinizer trees in the orchard. It also varies from region to region, and from year to year, depending on the presence of wild pollinators and honey bees, the weather, tree size and flowering patterns, planting distance, etc. Despite this variability, approximately 250 nesting females are sufficient to fully pollinate an acre of apples, and 300 to pollinate an acre of almonds. To account for potential dispersal and mortality of pre-nesting females, the actual number of females that should be released is higher. In fact, 10 to 20 percent more females should be added if natal nests are used, and some 40 to 50 percent if bees are released from loose cocoons. The number of males released should be 1.5 to 2 times that of females.

Orchards normally can support BOB populations larger than those strictly necessary for optimal pollination. Having more than 250 to 300 females established per acre will not result in better fruit yields, but may result in more bee progeny produced. However, adding extra females to a particular orchard should be done with caution. Releasing populations too large for the available bloom can cause high pre-nesting female dispersal. At the same time, if more bees establish than the orchard can support, pollen-nectar resources will become scarce. Under these circumstances, BOB females supply their nests with small provisions and lay mostly male eggs. Brood mortality increases with small body size and/or insufficient nectar being deposited in the provisions. Yearly alternating flower producing patterns, typical of many fruit tree cultivars, should also be considered when deciding managed BOB population sizes.

5.4. Advancing Emergence for Almond Pollination

Almonds are the earliest-flowering fruit trees. In California's Central Valley, they generally bloom in February. Wild BOBs from the central California foothills (600–1,100 feet [200–350 m] elevation) fly in March or April, at least a month later than almond bloom. Populations from colder areas, such as northern Utah, fly even later, in April or May. The easiest way to pollinate California almonds with BOBs would be to establish and rear February-flying populations. To establish later-flying populations in California almond orchards, bee emergence needs to be advanced by one to three months. To accomplish this, three different methods have been tested:

1) Late-flying BOB populations can be removed from wintering conditions one month ahead of expected bloom and incubated at 84°F (29°C). After being exposed to a short wintering period, the bees will have an extended emergence period. Bees emerging early need to be placed under wintering conditions until the whole population

has emerged. Then, the whole population can be released. This method ensures perfect synchrony with bloom initiation. However, bees need to be released as emerged adults, which increases dispersal of pre-nesting females (see section 5.2).

2) BOB development can be shortened by exposing bees to fluctuating temperatures (57:81 °F [14:27 °C]) during the developmental period. Because they reach adulthood ahead of their natural life cycle (Figure 24, page 27), populations reared in this way can be wintered earlier in the year to accumulate some 150 wintering days by early February. By using this method, late-flying (April to May), populations can be managed to emerge over a relatively short period in early February. Similar results can be obtained by rearing late-flying BOBs at 84 °F (29 °C) (Figure 24, page 27), although at this temperature mortality during development and wintering is slightly higher than at 57:81 °F (14:27 °C) (Table 3, page 29).

3) BOB emergence periods also can be shortened using milder wintering temperatures. Late-flying male BOBs from northern Utah wintered for 150 days take 3.5 days on average to emerge when wintered at 39 °F (4 °C), versus 0.5 days when wintered at 45 °F (7 °C) (Figure 27, page 32).

The progeny of late-flying bees managed to emerge and nest earlier in the year maintain their original developmental rate, which means they are likely to become adults by early summer instead of late summer. For this reason, these bees cannot be reared under natural conditions in California almond-growing areas, as hot summer temperatures would cause pre-wintering adults to use up their fat body reserves. Instead, these bees can be reared artificially at a constant temperature (e.g., 72 °F [22 °C]) and, upon adulthood, wintered early to accumulate enough wintering days to emerge promptly by February of the following year. In other words, bees produced from manipulated populations during the first year can be used on almonds in subsequent years, as long as their development and wintering are kept artificially out of phase with the natural life cycle in their area of origin.

6

OTHER MANAGEMENT PRACTICES

BOB nesting periods often last longer than the flowering period of commercial orchards. Therefore, after petal fall of the orchard crop, a number of BOB females may still be actively nesting. If later-flowering fruit tree species or wild flowers are available in or near the orchard, BOB populations can be left in place to continue pollination and progeny production. However, in situations of extremely brief orchard bloom followed by no alternative pollen-nectar resources, it may be advisable to provide BOB females with supplemental floral sources. This can be accomplished by planting alternative pollen-nectar sources in the vicinity or within the orchard, or by moving the nesting BOB population to a new area with pollen-nectar sources. The first approach also should be considered when rearing BOB populations solely to increase their numbers — known as "bee ranching" or "bee farming"— not for pollination. The second approach is particularly appropriate in situations where post-bloom pesticide sprays threaten the nesting population.

6.1. Providing Alternative Pollen-Nectar Sources

An extended flowering period for managed BOB populations can be provided easily by releasing bees at sites where various fruit tree cultivars or species bloom consecutively. In commercial orchard environments, however, special attention should be given to pesticide application schedules for each crop. Wild flowers and weeds also can serve as acceptable pollen sources and should not be removed from the vicinity of the orchard, unless they jeopardize crop production. These alternative food sources do not compete with the target crop for BOB visits, as BOBs prefer fruit tree flowers.

Of special interest are plants that blossom at the beginning of orchard bloom. Dandelions (*Taraxacum officinale*) are frequently visited by males and early-emerging females before the target crop has started to flower (Figure 12, page 12). Other plants visited by BOBs in orchard environments include Oregon grape (*Mahonia repens*), choke cherry (*Prunus virginiana*), crabapples (*Malus* spp.), certain willows (*Salix* spp.), common chickweed (*Stellaria media*), and several mustards (Brassicaceae). Additional pollen and flower-visiting records are listed in Table 1 (page 13) and Appendix 1 (page 74), respectively. Supplementary floral resources can be planted around the orchard or as an understory. This practice is especially suitable in organic orchards, as well as those with minimal and/or carefully planned pesticide programs.

BOBs can be managed away from commercial orchards for the sole purpose of increasing population numbers. Ideally, BOB "ranching" or "farming" areas should be free of pesticide sprays and planted with host plants that provide abundant pollen and nectar, as well as longer flowering periods than are typically found in orchard environments. Bee ranchers emphasize bee production, rather than pollination, and routinely sell a portion of their bees, retaining a residual population for brood production the following year. Recent studies indicate that meadowfoam, *Limnanthes alba*, is a promising plant on which to ranch BOB populations.

6.2. Moving Active BOB Populations

Actively nesting BOB females tend to abscond when moved to a new site, and more research is needed on the procedures and costs associated with moving active BOB populations. Relocating nesting units and small nesting shelters usually results in all or most of the females interrupting their nesting activities and leaving the new nesting site.

However, 85 percent re-establishment has been obtained in populations moved in shelters provided with large visual landmarks (e.g., 8 × 8 feet [2.5 × 2.5 m] plywood sheets). BOB populations should be moved at night, when temperatures are cool and females are inside their nesting cavities. Nest cavity entrances should be covered with a non-adhesive material to prevent females from crawling out of the nests during transport. Nesting materials should be either transported within their nesting shelter, or relocated at the new site in a nesting shelter identical to the original one. Nesting units should be placed in the same position within the nesting shelter as at the original site, as females become disoriented and abscond if nesting units are swapped or inverted. As explained above, jostling nesting materials during transportation can dislodge eggs and young larvae, which then die.

7
FACTORS LIMITING BOB POPULATION GROWTH

In commercial orchards, a well-managed BOB population will lay two to four female eggs and five to eight male eggs per nesting female. In years with favorable weather and in orchards with long flowering periods or abundant alternative floral resources, BOB females can be expected to lay up to six females eggs during their lifetimes. Under a hypothetical no-mortality situation, this would represent a potential annual two- to six-fold increase in population size. In reality, several factors limit BOB population growth. The impact of these factors can be minimized through adequate management practices. In this section, we discuss bee losses due to dispersal of pre-nesting females, pesticide sprays, and developmental and wintering mortality. Parasites, predators, and pathogens of the BOB are discussed in section 8.

7.1. Pre-nesting Female Dispersal

Dispersal of pre-nesting females — females that nest away from the nesting shelters provided in the orchard — is a common cause of significant bee losses. As explained in section 5.2, the release method and the distribution of nesting materials within the orchard have a very significant effect on pre-nesting female dispersal. Higher establishment is to be expected when bees are released within natal nests and distributed evenly among numerous nesting sites across the orchard. Again, populations should not be released on windy or rainy days.

Excessive pre-nesting female dispersal occurs when BOBs are released in a habitat with scarce floral resources. This may result from releasing the population much before bloom initiation. Providing some early-blooming trees or other preferred pollen-nectar sources (see Table 1, page 13, and section 6.1) within or bordering the orchard helps mitigate this problem. Pre-nesting dispersal is also high if bees are released when bloom is already declining, or if the released population is too large for the available floral resources.

Although still under investigation, preliminary evidence suggests that the conditions to which bees are exposed throughout their development and wintering periods have a significant impact on establishment. Bees reared or wintered under sub-optimal temperature regimes, or that are otherwise stressed, seem more likely to disperse from the release site than those reared under optimal conditions. Because inadequate rearing regimes also affect bee vigor, in some cases it may be difficult to distinguish between actual pre-nesting dispersal and adult post-emergence mortality. Spraying of certain fungicides during the pre-nesting period causes BOB females to massively abscond (see section 7.2). These losses are often mistakenly attributed to natural pre-nesting dispersal.

7.2. Pesticide Sprays

The use of insecticides during bloom should be avoided to prevent poisoning pollinating insects in general and BOBs in particular. If spraying is absolutely necessary, it is important to select insecticides with low bee toxicity and short-residual effects. Applications should be made in the evening, after bee activity has ended for the day. Information on the toxicity of different insecticides to the BOB is very limited. Although tolerance to various pesticides differs between bee species, chemicals that are highly toxic to honey bees usually are toxic to other bees. It is important to note that application of insecticides at sublethal doses may adversely affect nesting behavior, brood and cell production rates, and increase immature mortality. The same is true for certain fungicide applications. Following these applications, pre-nesting BOB females abscond. Already established females interrupt their nesting activities and spend unusually long periods inside their nests, despite favorable foraging conditions. These females typically act disoriented and hover around their nesting shelter, rarely collecting pollen or nectar. Cell production rates diminish dramatically, and the few cells built contain unusually small provisions. BOB populations thus treated dwindle very rapidly.

To avoid poisoning, BOB nesting shelters with active adults can be removed from the orchard prior to pesticide application and stored at a cool temperature ($<46°F$ [$<8°C$]) for up to four days without any consequences to bee survival. It is very important to relocate the nesting shelter to the exact position as before the treatment, so females will not be disoriented and will be able to resume normal nesting. For the same reason, the distribution of nesting units within the shelter should not be altered. Once nests are plugged, BOB immatures are effectively protected from pesticide applications.

7.3. Developmental and Winter Mortality

In any BOB population, a number of individuals fail to reach the adult stage due to mechanical damage, inadequate temperature and/or humidity conditions, inadequate food supply, etc. This type of mortality, called developmental mortality, does not include developmental arrest due to other organisms, such as parasites, predators, and pathogens (discussed in section 8). In some cases, though, mortality caused by microorganisms (fungi, bacteria, viruses) may be difficult to differentiate from developmental mortality. Most developmental mortality occurs in the egg, early larval, and prepupal stages.

BOB eggs and young larvae easily detach from the provision if recently built nests are not handled with sufficient care. The dislodged larva is unable to anchor to the pollen-nectar mass and can die of starvation. A similar situation occurs when the larva is physically unable to feed on the hardened surface of a dry provision because the mother bee was not able to collect sufficient nectar. Dry provisions also can result when nesting materials wick humidity away from the provision. On the other hand, eggs and young larvae may die when provisions are too moist, or when nests get wet or are kept in excessively humid environments. In these cases, mold proliferates both inside the cell and on the surface of paper straws. Finally, rearing temperatures also have a profound effect on developmental mortality (Table 3, page 29). In populations left undisturbed under adequate conditions, developmental mortality should be no higher than 5 percent.

In populations reared at insufficiently warm temperatures, some individuals remain in the prepupal dormant stage for abnormally extended periods (up to six months) without dying, in a state called prepupal developmental arrest. These individuals have to be wintered as live prepupae rather than adults and, although some survive the winter, they do not develop into healthy adults. Warmer or fluctuating temperature regimes during the summer decrease the incidence of prepupal developmental arrest. For instance, populations from northern Utah have about 17 percent prepupal developmental arrest when reared at 65°F (18°C) versus none when reared at 72°F (22°C). In agreement with their warmer temperature requirements, populations from central Texas have about 30 percent prepupal developmental arrest when reared at 72°F (22°C).

Some individuals reach the adult stage by late summer or fall, but fail to emerge the following spring. This is called winter mortality. Adults kept unchilled for long periods use up their metabolic reserves and tend to die during the winter. Excessively warm winter temperatures have a similar effect. High winter mortality also occurs when bees are chilled on time, but wintered too briefly. In this case, high winter mortality would be accompanied by an excessively prolonged emergence period. If bees are artificially wintered for too long, some individuals will emerge within the cooling unit, but most of them die in their cocoons. BOBs also will emerge within the cooling unit if winter temperatures are too warm (e.g., 50°F [10°C]). For the same reason, BOBs from northern Utah cannot be wintered at 45°F (7°C) for periods much longer than 150 days (Figure 27, page 32). Table 3 (page 29) shows how inadequate rearing regimes not only affect developmental mortality, but also winter mortality. In any case, larger individuals are more likely to survive the winter than smaller ones. In populations wintered under optimal conditions, no more than 5 percent winter mortality should be expected.

Inadequate rearing and/or wintering regimes may not cause mortality directly during development or wintering, but may affect bee vigor at emergence. Sometimes, bees kept as unchilled adults for too long in the fall are able to survive the winter, but are not vigorous enough to chew their way out of their cocoons in the spring. These individuals can be found dead in partially chewed cocoons in subsequent nest inspections. Other inadequately chilled individuals are able to emerge from their cocoons, but act sluggish and/or have difficulty flying. In severe cases, many of these bees eventually die without nesting, even if they gain access to a nectar source.

8

PARASITES, PREDATORS, AND PATHOGENS

Several parasites, predators, and pathogens prey on BOBs and related species. The impact of these BOB enemies varies widely from region to region and year to year. Although losses to parasites, predators, and pathogens are inevitable, infestation in managed BOB populations usually can be kept to acceptable levels. In this section, we provide information on how to identify the most common BOB enemies, with a brief description of their natural history. Control methods, when available, also are discussed. Some of the control methods may appear labor-intensive, but given the small numbers of BOBs needed to pollinate fruit trees, these methods can be implemented without excessive effort.

8.1. Chalcid Wasps, *Monodontomerus* spp.

Monodontomerus chalcid wasps (Hymenoptera: Torymidae), including *M. obscurus* and *M. montivagus*, are among the most common insects associated with the BOB. Adults of these parasitic wasps are metallic dark green to black, with red eyes (Figure 30, page 52). Males are about 0.08–0.12 inches (2–3 mm) long. Females are larger (0.12–0.16 inches [3–4 mm]), and have a long egg-laying organ (ovipositor) at the tip of their abdomen. Females use the ovipositor to pierce the bee cocoon and lay about 10 eggs on the bee prepupa or pupa. *Monodontomerus* larvae (0.12–0.2 inches [3–5 mm] long) consume all or most of the bee larva (Figure 31, page 52) and then pupate within the bee cocoon. Development from egg to adult lasts about one month, so two to four generations of the parasitic wasp may be produced during the summer. Each female may parasitize several bee cocoons. Adult *Monodontomerus* emerge through round holes (approximately 0.04 inches [1 mm] in diameter) that they chew in the BOB cocoon and nest walls. *Monodontomerus* winter as fully grown larvae inside the bee cocoon.

Monodontomerus infestations may build up throughout the summer and reach high levels unless managed appropriately. Because *Monodontomerus* adults only become active toward the end of the BOB nesting period, it is very important to remove nesting materials from the orchard or garden shortly before or immediately after nesting has finished to avoid or minimize initial infestation.

Another protection against *Monodontomerus* parasitism is to reduce accessibility of BOB cells after nests are stored for the developmental period (spring-summer). Mosquito screen (mesh size smaller than 0.04 inches [1 mm]) can be used to isolate *Monodontomerus*-free nests. Certain nesting materials provide better protection against *Monodontomerus* attack than others. *Monodontomerus* females readily oviposit through paper straws that have been removed from nesting blocks. Unprotected straws, especially in nesting materials such as milk cartons or other hollow nesting units, may suffer heavy infestation because parasitic wasps freely move from nest to nest. However, because *Monodontomerus* females cannot oviposit through cardboard tubes with walls thicker than 0.04 inches (1 mm), parasitism can be minimized by using paper tubes inserted in cardboard tubes. For the same reason, nests produced in reeds are well protected against *Monodontomerus* wasps. Paper straws left within solid nesting blocks are unlikely to be heavily parasitized.

Monodontomerus females are opportunistic and may readily find and parasitize the innermost cells of nests (even through the initial mud partition), as well as accessible cells in uncompleted (uncapped) nests. Double-sided tape or some other type of physical barrier covering the back and the entrance of BOB nests help reduce accessibility of these cells. Loose cocoons attract *Monodontomerus* females in great numbers and suffer heavy mortality unless protected by a screen or other means. Cocoons of the alfalfa leafcutting bee, *Megachile rotundata*, are sometimes covered with sawdust or vermiculite as a protection against *Monodontomerus* and other parasitic wasps.

Finally, black light traps installed in the storage area for BOB populations attract and kill *Monodontomerus* wasps in large numbers. A simple black light trap is shown in Figure 32. *Monodontomerus* adults are attracted to the ultraviolet light of the fluorescent bulb and drowned in a tray containing baby oil or water with a few drops of detergent.

8.2. Chalcid Wasp, *Melittobia chalybii*

Melittobia chalybii (Hymenoptera: Eulophidae) is a less common chalcid wasp found in BOB nests. The adults of this parasitic wasp measure only about 0.04–0.06 inches (1–1.5 mm). *Melittobia* females are dark brown to black (Figure 33) and typically hop when disturbed. Males, which are much less numerous than females, are pale brown and have short wings. Adult females chew holes to gain access to brood cells, where they lay several egg batches on the bee larva or pupa. More than 100 parasitic wasp larvae may feed on a single bee larva. Fully grown *M. chalybii* larvae measure about 0.04–0.06 inches (1–1.5 mm). Development of *M. chalybii* from egg to adult requires about 20 days, so several re-infesting generations may occur throughout the summer. Exiting adult wasps chew small holes through the nest walls. Wintering occurs in the last larval stage.

Because of their flattened shape, *M. chalybii* females gain access to nests through tiny gaps in nesting materials. Furthermore, *M. chalybii* are able to chew through a number of materials, including mud, cardboard, and plastic, and ultraviolet light traps used to control *Monodontomerus* wasps are ineffective against *M. chalybii*. However, the BOB is not a frequent host of *M. chalybii*, which is more commonly found in nests of later-flying *Osmia* species (especially those using masticated leaf materials instead of mud to build their nests plugs), and some solitary wasps. In most cases, removing BOB nests at the end of the nesting period and isolating them from nests of other hosts should maintain *M. chalybii* parasitism at low levels.

Figure 30. Adult female chalcid wasp, *Monodontomerus*, ovipositing in blue orchard bee cocoon. Note long ovipositor sheath at tip of the abdomen.

Figure 31. Infested blue orchard bee cocoon opened to show *Monodontomerus* larvae.

Figure 32. Blue orchard bee nests by black light trap. Note large numbers of drowned *Monodontomerus* in tray.

Figure 33. Adult female chalcid wasp, *Melittobia chalybii*.

Figure 34. Adult chalcid wasp, *Leucospis affinis*.

8.3. Chalcid Wasp, *Leucospis affinis*

Another chalcid wasp, *Leucospis affinis* (Hymenoptera: Leucospidae), is occasionally found attacking BOB nests. Adults of this large parasite (Figure 34) measure 0.3–0.4 inches (8–10 mm), have enlarged hind legs, and show distinct black-and-yellow color patterns. Females use their very long ovipositor to lay eggs in the bee cocoons. Because *L. affinis* females can pierce through wood, BOB nests in holes drilled less than 0.75 inches (2 cm) from the edge of a wood block are susceptible to attack. The parasitic larva feeds on the host prepupa. *Leucospis affinis* larvae pupate within the host cocoon without spinning cocoons of their own. Only one parasite develops per cell. *Leucospis affinis* can have more than one generation per year and winter as prepupae. *Leucospis affinis* infestations usually are not serious and can be avoided by storing nesting materials soon after the nesting period.

Figure 35. Adult chrysidid wasp, *Chrysura*.

Figure 36. Adult sapygid wasp, *Sapyga*.

Figure 37. Sapygid wasp, *Sapyga*, cocoons. Note aggregations of white particles on basal (left) half of the cocoon and brown fecal particles.

8.4. Chrysidid Wasps, *Chrysura* spp.

Several chrysidid wasps (Hymenoptera: Chrysididae) in the genus *Chrysura*, *C. smaragdicolor* and *C. pacifica* in the western United States, and *C. kyrae* in the eastern part of the country, prey on the BOB. Adults of these *Chrysura* (Figure 35) are green to blue metallic in color and measure about 0.3–0.5 inches [8–12 mm] in length. *Chrysura* females enter BOB nests when the BOB female is away foraging and lay their eggs on the side of the pollen-nectar provision. The wasp larva, which has a distinctive forked tail, attaches to the back or side of the BOB larva. Eventually, the chrysidid wasp larva molts and devours the full-grown bee larva. It then spins a thin transparent cocoon (brown with a typical white patch), sometimes within the already spun bee cocoon. In BOB nests, *Chrysura* winter as adults and have one generation per year.

8.5. Sapygid Wasp, *Sapyga* sp.

The sapygid wasp, *Sapyga* sp. (Hymenoptera: Sapygidae), is a cleptoparasite, meaning the larva consumes the bee provision, not the bee itself. Adults of *Sapyga* sp. (Figure 36) are black with yellow patterns. They measure about 0.3–0.6 inches [8–14 mm] in length. Females lay their eggs in sealed cells and, although they may lay more than one egg per cell, only one offspring develops. The young cleptoparasitic wasp larva kills the bee egg and feeds on the provision. The last-stage wasp larva completes consumption of the BOB provision, then spins a cocoon prior to pupation. *Sapyga* sp. winter as adults inside their cocoons. Their cocoons are similar to BOB cocoons, but usually are more slender, darker, and have some minute (0.02–0.04 inches [0.5–1 mm] long) cylindrical particles of whitish anal secretion on the outside (Figure 37). *Sapyga* sp. have one generation per year.

Sapyga sp. is a relatively common cleptoparasite of the BOB. Night station traps are commercially available to control a related sapygid, *Sapyga pumila*, that parasitizes the alfalfa leafcutting bee, *Megachile rotundata*. Basically, night station traps are PVC cylinders with several 0.1-inch-diameter (2.5-mm-diameter) holes and fitted inside with a sticky cardboard strip (Figure 38). Because *S. pumila* adults select cavi-

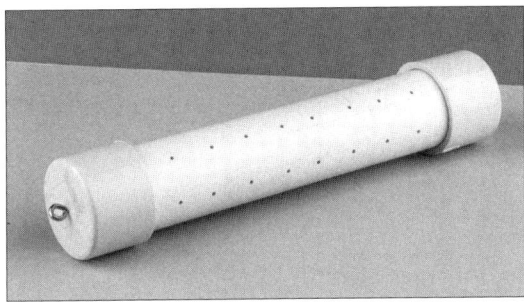

Figure 38. Sapygid wasp, *Sapyga pumila*, night station trap. Note small holes to attract *S. pumila* adults.

ties of that diameter to spend the night, they are attracted to night station traps and become stuck on the sticky strips. Night station traps are installed on alfalfa leafcutting bee nesting shelters during the nesting period. To test the potential effectiveness of night station traps as a control method against *Sapyga* sp., hole diameters would likely have to be modified to accommodate the larger-sized *Sapyga* sp. adults.

8.6. Cuckoo bee, *Stelis montana*

The cuckoo bee, *Stelis montana* (Hymenoptera: Megachilidae), is another cleptoparasite commonly associated with the BOB. Cuckoo bee adults (Figure 39) are similar in color and appearance to BOB adults. They are, however, slightly smaller (0.3–0.4 inches [8–10 mm]) long, lack white facial hairs, and females lack the pollen-carrying organ (scopa). Female *S. montana* lay their eggs in uncapped BOB and related *Osmia* cells, while the nesting female is away foraging. The cuckoo bee larva kills the *Osmia* larva and consumes about three-quarters of the pollen-nectar provision. *Stelis montana* has only one generation per year and winters as a prepupa inside the cocoon. Only one cuckoo bee develops in each parasitized BOB cell. Parasitized cells can be distinguished by the distinct cuckoo bee cocoon and fecal particles (Figure 40). The cuckoo bee fecal particles are long and curly, and cocoons have a more prominent nipple and are much harder (difficult to squeeze between two fingers) than those of the BOB. *Stelis montana* cocoons can be detected by inspecting BOB nests in semi-translucent paper straws against a light bulb. Infested straws can be dissected and cuckoo bee cocoons removed.

Figure 39. Adult cuckoo bee, *Stelis montana*.

Figure 40. Cuckoo bee, *Stelis montana*, cocoons. Note prominent nipple (right) and curly fecal particles.

8.7. Blister Beetle, *Tricrania stansburyi*

The blister beetle, *Tricrania stansburyi* (Coleoptera: Meloidae), is a third cleptoparasite of the BOB. The adults of this blister beetle (Figure 41) are black with blood-red wing covers and measure about 0.4-0.5 inches (10–12 mm) long. Females lay their eggs on or near flowering plants. When eggs hatch, the first larval stage (triungulin) crawls atop a flower, where it waits for the visit of a potential bee host. When a female BOB visits a flower with triungulins present, one or more grasp the bee's leg hairs. In this way, triungulins are transported to a BOB nest and introduced to a cell being provisioned. After the cell is sealed, the triungulin punctures the BOB egg, and in later larval stages consumes the BOB pollen-nectar provision. *Tricrania stansburyi* have only one generation per year. Normally, the adult stage of the blister beetle is produced by late summer and remains in the BOB cell, enclosed within two translucent brown larval skins (Figure 42), until emergence the following spring. However, some *T. stansburyi* winter as pupae or larvae. Only one individual blister beetle develops per BOB cell. Because emergence tends to occur during the second half of the BOB nesting

Figure 41. Adult blister beetle, *Tricrania stansburyi*.

Figure 42. Wintering adult blister beetle, *Tricrania stansburyi*, enclosed within larval skins.

period, parasitism levels are usually higher in later-flying *Osmia* species. As with the cuckoo bee, *S. montana, T. stansburyi*-infested cells can be identified and removed from BOB nests within paper straws.

8.8. Checkered Flower Beetle, *Trichodes ornatus*

The checkered flower beetle, *Trichodes ornatus* (Coleoptera: Cleridae), is commonly associated with cavity-nesting bees. Adults of the checkered flower beetle (Figure 43) measure 0.3–0.6 inches (7–15 mm). They are metallic dark blue, with extensive bright yellow to reddish orange patterning on the wing covers. Females lay their eggs near the entrance of bee nests. The first larval stage measures about 0.08 inches (2 mm) and is creamy to salmon pink in color. Later stages may be as large as 0.5 inches (13 mm) and are salmon pink to scarlet. All larval stages have two characteristic spine-like processes at the tip of the abdomen (Figure 44). The first three larval stages feed on bee eggs or larvae as well as on pollen provisions. By going from cell to cell, they usually destroy the whole bee nest. Most individuals winter as fourth-stage larvae after building a chamber with thin partitions of brown semi-transparent

Figure 43. Adult checkered flower beetle, *Trichodes ornatus*.

Figure 44. Checkered flower beetle, *Trichodes ornatus*, fully grown larva. Note forked spiny process at the tip of the abdomen (left).

Figure 45. Checkered flower beetle, *Trichodes ornatus*, trap opened to show trapped beetles, attracted with a scent bait.

oral secretion. In the spring, one or two more larval stages occur prior to pupation and adulthood. Some individuals spend two or three years as larvae. Removing BOB nesting materials from the orchard or garden shortly before or immediately after the end of the nesting period and storing BOBs away from nests of other late-flying cavity nesting bees help avoid infestation. Checkered flower beetles attack also nests of the alfalfa leafcutting bee. Commercially available traps (Figure 45) consist of a plastic container with a pheromone-impregnated capsule that attracts adult checkered flower beetles during the alfalfa leafcutting bee nesting period.

8.9. Spider Beetle, *Ptinus californicus*

Adults of the spider beetle, *Ptinus californicus* (Coleoptera: Ptinidae), measure about 0.2 inches (5 mm) in length (Figure 46). They are brown, with four irregular transverse white patches on the wing covers, and have long antennae. *Ptinus californicus* have only one generation per year. Females lay their eggs in or near unsealed BOB cells. Up to four or five *P. californicus* larvae may develop in a BOB cell, where they consume the provision, sometimes starving the bee larva. When only one or two beetle larvae are present in a cell, both the spider beetle and the BOB may survive. Besides pollen and nectar, the grub-like spider beetle larvae feed on other nest components, including bee feces, cocoons and bee corpses. In so doing, they may injure or kill both immature and mature bees. Infested cells have distinctive, abundant masses of long fecal strings (Figure 47). The last-stage larva uses a shiny adhesive secretion to build a chamber among the fecal material or against the BOB cell wall. Pupation, adulthood, and wintering occur within this chamber. Most individuals winter as adults, but some as pupae or larvae. Emergence holes made by *P. californicus* on the walls of BOB nests in paper straws are similar to those made by *Monodontomerus*, but larger and more irregular. Some *P. californicus* emerge through the BOB nest plug. *Ptinus californicus* is normally not a serious threat to BOB populations, and appears to act mostly as an opportunistic scavenger. However, as with carpet beetles and flour beetles (see below), spider beetles should be eliminated from incubation trays or nesting materials whenever possible.

8.10. Carpet Beetles, Dermestidae

Several carpet beetles, *Trogoderma* spp., *Attagenus* spp., *Anthrenus* spp., and *Megatoma* spp. (Coleoptera: Dermestidae), are relatively common scavengers in BOB nests. Adults measure 0.1 inches (3 mm) or less, and are usually oval, brown or black, with tan or white patterns on the wing covers (Figure 48). They usually lay their eggs in uncapped cells, or in the innermost cell of nests that have broken or missing initial mud partitions. Fully grown larvae are about 0.2 inches (5 mm) long, reddish brown, with long bristles (Figure 49). Carpet beetles winter in all stages and have several generations per year. They feed on pollen-nectar provisions and other nest debris. Carpet beetles may enter cocoons and injure immature and mature bees.

8.11. Flour Beetles, *Tribolium* spp.

Flour beetles, *Tribolium* spp. (Coleoptera: Tenebrionidae), are another group of scavengers found in BOB nests. *Tribolium* adults are elongated, brown with grooved wing covers (Figure 50), and measure 0.12–0.25 inches (3–6 mm). They lay their eggs on accessible pollen provisions and have several generations per year. The larvae are light brown, with dark brown bands across the body (Figure 51). Flour beetles are scavengers, but may injure host bees. As with spider and carpet beetles, flour beetles usually do not cause serious mortality levels in BOB populations.

8.12. Hairy-fingered Mite, *Chaetodactylus krombeini*

Hairy-fingered mites (also known as pollen mites), *Chaetodactylus krombeini* (Acari: Chaetodactylidae), are common cleptoparasites of the BOB. Adult mites (Figure 52A) are white, ovoid and very small (males: 450 microns; females: 600 microns). Adult female mites lay many eggs in BOB cells. Mite immatures (larvae and nymphs) measure 250–450 microns, and feed on the provision's pollen grains. The bee egg is either punctured by mites or the young bee larva starves. Occasionally, the immature bee is not killed, in which case a smaller-than-normal adult bee may develop, along with some mites. Mites are not able to break through intact cell partitions, but frequently move into adjacent cells when partitions break during nest manipulation.

Figure 47. Spider beetle, *Ptinus californicus*, larva in blue orchard bee cell. Note abundant spider beetle fecal particles.

Figure 46. Adult spider beetle, *Ptinus californicus*.

Figure 49. Carpet beetle larva. Note long bristles on each segment.

Figure 48. Adult carpet beetle, *Trogoderma*.

Several generations occur within each infested cell. By the end of the summer, the infested cell is packed with loose, dry, empty pollen grains and thousands of mites (Figure 53). Mites may develop into either migratory or non-migratory second-stage nymphs. Migratory nymphs are distinguishable from other stages because they are flatter and have two reddish-brown triangular dorsal plates and three very long bristles at the end of their hind legs (Figure 52B). In the following spring, some adult BOBs have to chew through infested cells to emerge from the nest. At this point, migratory nymphs cling to the bee's hairs and are transported to other nesting cavities. Sometimes, mites can be clearly seen covering parts of the bee's body (Figure 54). Non-migratory mite nymphs are white and globular and have no functional legs (Figure 52C). They remain encased in the skin of the previous developmental stage (first-stage nymph) within their natal cell. In the spring,

Figure 50. Adult flour beetle, *Tribolium*. Note grooves on wing covers.

Figure 51. Flour beetle, *Tribolium*, larva. Note dark bands on each segment.

non-migratory nymphs may reinfest the cavity where they were produced, if a BOB female uses it to nest, or they may turn into migratory nymphs.

Parasitism by *C. krombeini* can attain high levels, especially in humid areas. Inspection of BOB nests in semi-translucent paper straws and removal of infested cells is a time-consuming, but effective, method to prevent damaging *C. krombeini* infestations. Stripping BOB cocoons out of the nesting materials and managing loose cocoons, instead of whole nests, reduces initial infestation because emerging BOBs are not forced to

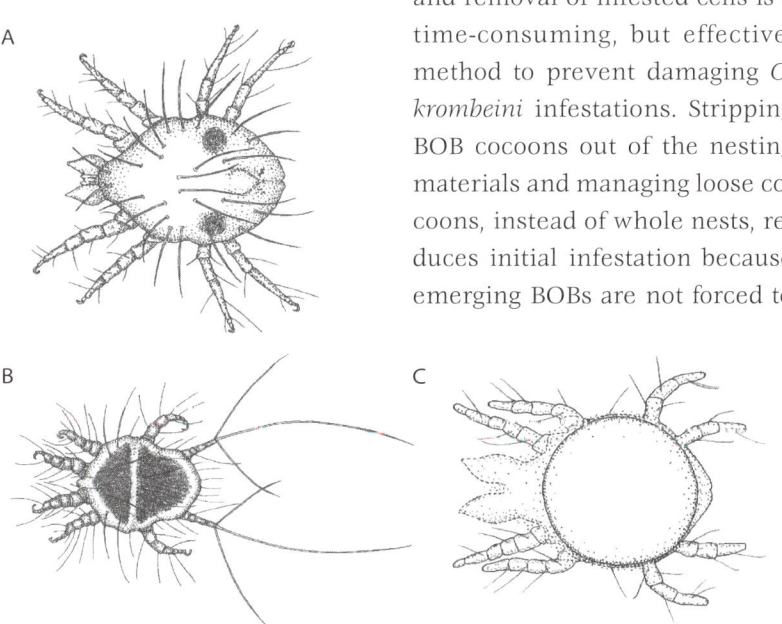

Figure 52A, B, and C. Developmental stages of the hairy-fingered mite, *Chaetodactylus krombeini*. **A.** Adult. **B.** Migratory nymph with dark dorsal plates and long bristles at the tip of hind legs. **C.** Globular, legless non-migratory nymph within skin of first-stage nymph.

walk through infested cells. However, as discussed in section 5.2, releasing BOB populations as loose cocoons increases dispersal of pre-nesting females.

Studies on the Japanese species *Chaetodactylus nipponicus*, associated with the hornfaced bee, *Osmia cornifrons*, show significant reductions of mite infestation in nesting materials treated with endosulfan (60–600 ppm). These same studies indicate that exposure of hornfaced bee nests to high temperatures (e.g., 60 days at 86°F [30°C], or three days at 104°F [40°C]) effectively kills *C. nipponicus* mites without harming hornfaced bees, as long as the bees are in the prepupal stage. The potential utility of these or similar methods to control *C. krombeini* in BOB populations is being tested.

8.13. Chalkbrood, *Ascosphaera* spp.

The genus *Ascosphaera* (Ascomycetes: Ascosphaerales) includes several species of pathogenic fungi, commonly known as chalkbrood, that attack bee larvae. The most common species to attack BOBs, *Ascosphaera torchioi*, is different from the chalkbrood species found on alfalfa leafcutting bees or honey bees. BOB larvae become infested when they ingest chalkbrood spores from contaminated pollen-nectar provisions. Chalkbrood spores germinate inside the gut of the BOB larva, and produce long filaments (hyphae) that eventually penetrate the internal wall of the gut, causing the death of the larva. In most cases, new chalkbrood spores are produced at the tips of the hyphae, just below the skin of the BOB larval cadaver. Some infested BOB larvae die after consuming the pollen-nectar provision during cocoon spinning. These larvae typically show a continuous layer of dark chalkbrood spore aggregations throughout the body (Figure 55). Other BOB larvae die before consuming the whole provision; these larvae are usually only partially filled with spore aggregations. When an adult BOB female chews her way through a nest cell that contains a chalkbrood-infested cadaver, she becomes dusted with spores. These spores may be deposited on pollen-nectar provisions as the BOB builds her nest.

To reduce chalkbrood levels, BOB immatures should be reared at adequate temperatures (see Table 3, page 29, Figure 24, page 27, and section 4.2). Temperatures that slow BOB development delay larval defecation, increasing the likelihood that chalkbrood spores will germinate inside the larva's gut. As with *C. krombeini* mites, inspection of BOB nests and removal of infested cells is a simple way to further reduce chalkbrood incidence. Using loose cocoons reduces chalkbrood levels because emerging bees do not have to chew through infested cadavers, but also increases unwanted dispersal of pre-nesting BOB females. Because chalkbrood spores remain viable for years, using new nesting cavities (paper straws, reeds) is an essential measure for chalkbrood control. Alternatively, certain nesting materials (wood blocks, grooved boards) can be sanitized by submerging nesting materials in a solution of household bleach (6 percent sodium hypochlorite) and water (1:3 by volume) for five minutes. This procedure is used to manage chalkbrood in alfalfa leafcutting bee populations.

8.14. Birds, Rodents, and Ants

Certain birds (robins, starlings, crows, woodpeckers) prey on adult BOBs as they emerge from their nests. BOBs are especially vulnerable in the early morning hours, when bees bask on the surface of the nesting materials before starting their first foraging trip. Bird damage can be serious if no control is implemented. Placing chicken wire (1.5 inch [37 mm] mesh) in front of the nest entrances (Figure 21, page 23) provides good protection against bird attacks and does not deter BOB females from freely flying in and out of their nests. Acetylene-powered cannons are another effective method to keep birds at bay.

Rodents, including mice (*Peromyscus* spp.) and gray squirrels (*Sciurus griseus*), also prey upon BOBs. Rodents can learn to pull out straws from nesting materials and feed on the pollen-nectar provisions and bee larvae. As with birds, chicken wire provides good protection. Another way to hinder mouse access to a nesting shelter is to apply sticky barriers (e.g., tanglefoot) or insert inverted pie pans on the legs of the shelter. Mice also may destroy BOB nests while these are stored during the summer and winter.

Fire ants, *Solenopsis invicta*, and Argentine ants, *Linepithema humile*, sometimes raid BOB nests, both during the nesting period and during the storage period. Sticky barriers are a useful deterrent against ant attacks.

Figure 53. Infested blue orchard bee cell showing disintegrated pollen-nectar provision and thousands of hairy-fingered mites, *Chaetodactylus krombeini*.

Figure 54. Recently emerged male blue orchard bee covered with hairy-fingered mite, *Chaetodactylus krombeini*, migratory nymphs.

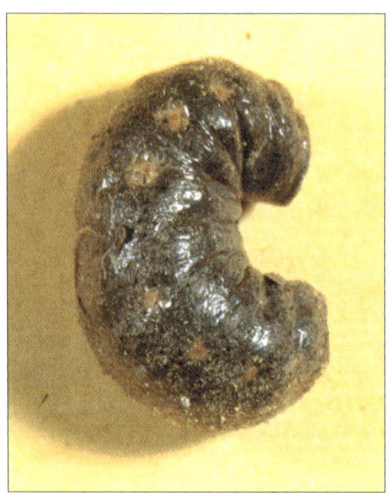 

Figure 55. Blue orchard bee larvae infested with chalkbrood, *Ascosphaera*. The cuticle of the right larva has been broken to show the accumulation of black, microscopic spore aggregations.

9

HOW TO QUANTIFY BOB POPULATIONS

The average number of cells per nest, sex ratio, and percent progeny mortality in BOB populations vary widely between years, nesting environments, and nesting materials. For this reason, simply counting the number of nests in a managed BOB population provides a poor estimate of the actual number of male and female progeny. To obtain a reliable estimate, it is necessary to carefully examine the contents of a random sample of 40 to 50 nests. If different nesting materials are being used, it is important to include nests from each material in the survey. Nest interiors can be easily observed by opening grooved boards, splitting reed sections, or slicing paper tubes. To avoid damaging progeny, it is best to inspect nests after cocoon spinning. Semi-translucent paper straws permit acceptable "reading" of the nest contents when observed against a strong light. As explained in section 4.2, nesting materials can also be X-rayed (Figures 25 and 26, pages 28 and 30).

Most cells are easy to sex by size and position, and sex counts should be 90-percent accurate. As explained, female individuals are typically produced in the innermost cells and are larger than male cells (Figures 5, 9, and 25, pages 7, 11, and 28). However, some intermediate-sized cocoons may be difficult to assign to either sex, and, occasionally, nests may contain one or more distinctly large cocoons (females) located after distinctly small cocoons (male).

Cells with dead eggs or larvae, and most parasitized cells, can be easily identified (see section 8) and deducted from the counts. Cells with dead prepupae, pupae, or adults cannot be identified unless the cocoons are dissected or X-rayed. However, dead prepupae, pupae, and adults should be uncommon if populations are reared following the directions provided in this manual.

Populations are best analyzed in the fall, when bees are completely developed. Live bees still in the prepupal or pupal stages at the time populations require wintering (late summer or early fall) are an indication of insufficiently warm rearing temperatures. Those individuals should be considered non-viable because they die during the winter or, if they survive, are unable to develop into healthy adults by the following spring. Wintering adult mortality should be deducted from fall counts, but wintering mortality should be less than 5 percent if populations are reared and wintered properly.

Bee return estimates (comparison between progeny population obtained versus parental population released), should be based on live female counts, rather than on live bee (males + females) counts. As discussed in previous sections, several sub-optimal situations, such as scarcity of pollen-nectar resources, inadequate nesting materials, poor female vigor, etc., result in highly male-biased sex ratios. Females pollinate many more flowers than males, and, because only females construct and provision nests, extra males in a population (more than two males per female) will not result in higher bee production. In other words, increasing the number of male BOBs has little value unless accompanied by an increased number of females.

10

HOW TO OBTAIN BOB POPULATIONS

For those who do not require large BOB populations (e.g., backyard gardeners), and reside in areas where BOBs are abundant locally, setting out nesting materials may be a good way to attract sufficient numbers of females in just a few seasons. For large agricultural operations there are two ways to start BOB populations: trap-nesting for wild populations or purchasing commercial populations. It is important to realize that the developing BOB industry cannot rely solely on trap-nesting as a source for bees, and repeated trap-nesting at a given site could deplete local wild populations. The BOB industry will only be sustainable if managed populations can be maintained or increased on a yearly basis. This can be accomplished either in orchard or garden environments, where populations are released for pollination, or in BOB-ranching areas, where populations are managed to increase their numbers (section 6.1).

10.1. Trap-nesting BOBs

The first step to trap-nesting is to locate areas where BOB populations occur naturally. There is no easy way to determine whether a particular site hosts wild BOB populations. Forested riparian areas offer potentially good sites because they are likely to provide natural nesting cavities (abandoned beetle burrows in dead wood). BOBs also require adequate pollen and nectar sources (see Table 1, page 13), as well as mud sources (creeks, springs, damp soil from snow melt, etc.) generally associated with riparian areas. However, those characteristics do not guarantee that BOBs will occur at a particular site. Sometimes, BOBs are abundant in urban areas, presumably taking advantage of cavities in wood beams, fences and other lumber. The presence of BOBs can be confirmed by netting and identifying bees on spring flowers, or setting out small numbers of trap-nests.

Trap-nests are essentially the same nesting materials used in orchard releases, but they are made to be tied, wired, or nailed to trees, stumps, or fence posts. Trap-nests should be set out shortly before the beginning of the BOB nesting season. BOB females searching for nesting cavities are likely to encounter trap-nests and, if the nesting materials are attractive, nest in them.

The spacing between trap-nests in a survey depends on the presumed BOB population density, the abundance of natural nesting cavities, and the number of cavities per trap-nest. It is advisable to place trap-nests inconspicuously to protect them from potential vandalism. In certain areas or years, rodents and birds may damage nesting materials. Recommendations to screen nesting materials given in section 8.14 are applicable to trap-nesting.

Trap-nests should be retrieved as soon as the BOB nesting period is over. Trap-nests left for long periods are likely to attract later-flying bee and wasp species, as well as BOB parasites and predators. Trap-nests should be handled carefully at this point to avoid killing eggs and young larvae, and should be stored with the cavity entrances facing up to avoid reverse cocoon spinning.

Most other bees and wasps that might nest in BOB trap-nests generally fly later in the season and use materials other than mud (such as masticated leaf, resin, pebbles, grass blades, leaf cuts, etc.) to cap their nests. Most nests of these species can be easily distinguished from BOB nests. However, some solitary wasps and *Osmia* species other than the BOB, particularly *Osmia californica*, also use mud to build nest plugs and cell partitions. Wasps usually produce nest plugs having a smoother appearance than those of BOBs. Wasp cocoons typically are attached to both the anterior and posterior cell partitions and are translucent and much thinner than BOB cocoons. Wasp cells are provisioned with paralyzed caterpillars or other insects, instead of pollen. *Osmia californica* nests are similar to BOB nests, but the nest plug is often slightly recessed (0.2–0.6 inches [0.5–1.5 cm]) within the nesting cavity, instead of flush with the cavity opening. Another difference between the two species is that *O. californica* females usually mix masticated leaf pulp with soil to build their nests. Small masticated leaf pieces can be detected on the plug and cell partitions with a hand lens. Unlike BOBs, *O. californica* females bury their eggs in the center of the provision, rather than laying them on the anterior provision surface. *Osmia californica* females collect pollen only from composite flowers, and their nests have a characteristic pungent smell. Furthermore, the outer walls of paper straws containing *O. californica* nests typically are stained yellow or orange from their pollen-nectar provisions. Like the BOB, *O. californica* cocoons are thick and opaque, but they are attached to both cell partitions, and have a series of translucent layers at their anterior end that hide the nipple. The fecal material of *O. californica* is typically yellow or orange, and some fecal particles are smeared against the outer layer of the cocoon.

Because BOBs produce one generation a year, trap-nested bees only can be used the following year. As mentioned previously, trap-nesting can be a good way to start or expand a managed population, but not to obtain new populations every year. Those interested in trap-nesting wild BOB populations should be aware that trapping is subject to local, state (or provincial), and federal land use regulations.

10.2. Purchasing BOBs

Commercial BOB populations are available in the United States and Canada. The Logan Bee Biology and Systematics Laboratory website (http://www.LoganBeeLab.usu.edu) contains a list of suppliers, most of which also sell nesting materials. Purchasers should be aware that the United States and Canada have different laws regulating shipment of bees across administrative borders. Information on appropriate procedures can be obtained from state or provincial Agriculture Departments.

Bees are shipped most safely as wintering adults in insulated containers, and should be shipped rapidly to avoid overexposure to warm temperatures. Before purchasing bees, it is important to obtain information on the bee stock. The BOB supplier should be able to provide information on the flying period of the parental generation, as well as the progeny rearing and wintering schedules. This information will help in predicting expected emergence dates, and remove a great deal of guesswork in managing the purchased BOB population.

Because BOB females do most of the pollination, the purchased population needs to have an acceptable sex ratio, the most optimal being 1.5 to 2 males per female. Higher male-biased sex ratios often indicate sub-optimal or stress conditions during nesting, such as poor weather, insufficient pollen and nectar sources, short or small-diameter nesting cavities, a high proportion of unmated females, etc. Few cells per nest, excessive developmental mortality, and small bees also indicate poor nesting conditions. Populations with less than one male per female are rarely encountered, but can result from interrupted nesting, poor weather during the second half of the nesting period (when most male cells are produced), or premature removal of nesting materials. Excessively female-biased sex ratios also can result from inadequate rearing regimes, such as excessively high temperatures, at a point in the life cycle in which males are more likely to die than females (females tend to develop at a slightly slower pace). In any case, populations with low male numbers should be supplemented with extra males. Otherwise, some of the released females may remain unmated, resulting in an even greater proportion of male progeny in the next generation.

Finally, it is critical to know whether the bee population is parasite free. If not, nests must be inspected and culled by the purchaser. Otherwise, limited BOB population growth due to reinfestation of parasites, predators, or diseases should be expected. Shipping uninspected nests also brings the risk of introducing parasites to new areas, with a serious potential threat to local populations of BOBs and other wild bee species.

11

CONCLUDING REMARKS

In this manual, we attempted to synthesize existing knowledge and outline the procedures and tools required to manage for pollination with the BOB and, at the same time, note areas where our knowledge needs to be expanded. Just as with honey bees, we expect that improved efficiency in BOB management will come from both continuing research and from innovative and observant practitioners. We hope the information we have provided in this manual will prove useful to both orchardists and beekeepers, and will interest a wide range of professional and amateur naturalists.

When rearing BOBs, it is important to realize that the basic steps are simple and required during just short periods. BOB management is further simplified by the small populations needed for sufficient pollination.

Based on our experience and on our interactions with people rearing BOBs commercially, the key factors to successful BOB management can be summarized as follows:

1) Nesting materials. Nest cavities should be 19/64 inches (7.5 mm) in diameter and no shorter than 6 inches (15 cm). Nesting materials should allow for easy nest inspection and mobility to constitute a true management system.

2) Rearing methods. Appropriate temperature regimes during the developmental and wintering periods will ensure good survival and emergence of vigorous bees. Populations of different geographical origin (and hence different phenology) require different temperature regimes, which also need to be adjusted according to the blooming period of the target crop. Although it is impossible to cover all potential scenarios in this book, we have tried to provide enough biological information to allow for regional or local customizing of BOB production. Rearing local BOB populations provides the most satisfactory results with the least amount of manipulation.
3) Release methods. BOB populations should be introduced in orchard environments as natal nests, with special attention given to timing of bee emergence and crop bloom. BOB populations also should be released in habitats with adequate floral resources. These practices will minimize dispersal of pre-nesting females.
4) Parasites. Routine prophylaxis and specific measures against locally abundant parasites, predators, and diseases are very important steps towards minimizing bee losses.

Using best management procedures, and barring BOB catastrophic losses to pesticides or to extreme weather (e.g., severe frosts or intensive rain throughout the entire flowering period of the target crop), excellent pollination and fruit set can be achieved. Depending on the weather during pollination, BOB population increases of 1.5- to five-fold can be obtained.

For those interested in using BOB populations for orchard pollination, we recommend starting with five acres or fewer. A first step might be to introduce small BOB populations into orchards already pollinated with honey bees. BOBs and honey bees peacefully coexist even when nesting next to each other. Once enough experience on BOB management has been gained, it will be possible to phase in BOB populations in increasingly larger portions of the orchard. Growers will see increases in pollination levels on those acres with BOB populations, especially in years with marginal weather conditions during bloom.

Many small- to medium-sized orchard producers can obtain more thorough, consistent, and reliable pollination with only a small investment in time and money. Besides achieving good fruit yields, those growers in areas with favorable conditions for BOB rearing will be able to steadily increase their BOB-pollinated acreage, or to sell excess BOBs.

Producers with large orchards are more likely to contract with custom pollinating companies. Custom pollinators who currently offer only honey bees will find that offering BOB populations can improve customer satisfaction through increased pollination. With an understanding of bees as foraging animals, together with knowledge and experience of medium- to large-scale pollination management challenges, it is very likely that "bee ranching" — or the production of BOB populations for later sale as pollinators — will emerge from the custom pollination sector first.

Because of the vagaries of late winter and spring weather, we recommend that those interested in large-scale BOB rearing provide sufficiently long flowering periods to their BOB populations. This can be accomplished by releasing bees in areas with sequentially flowering floral sources, or by releasing different parts of their BOB populations on different crops and/or geographical areas.

Finally, it is important to note that pollination is only one variable in the overall management system for orchard crops. Producers need to monitor pollination levels delivered by BOB populations early enough each season to either schedule for increases in water and fertilization (e.g., in cherries), or to thin (e.g., in apples) for maximum profitability. It is very likely that additional adjustments in orchard management will need to be investigated as BOBs are increasingly used as pollinators.

APPENDIX 1

Flower-Visiting Records of the Blue Orchard Bee

For confirmed pollen-collection records, see Table 1 on page 13.

PLANT FAMILY	SCIENTIFIC NAME	COMMON NAMES
Aceraceae	*Acer* sp.	Maple
Anacardiaceae	*Rhus trilobata* [=*Rhus aromatica* var. *trilobata*]	Ill-scented sumac; Three-lobed sumac
Apiaceae	*Erigenia* sp.	Harbinger of spring
	Osmorhiza sp.	Sweet Cicely; Sweetroot
	Taenidia sp.	Yellow pimpernel
Asteraceae	*Agoseris* sp.	Mountain dandelion; False dandelion
	Blemnosperma nanum	Common sticky seed
	Cirsium sp.	Thistle
	Geraea canescens	Hairy desert sunflower
	Senecio salignus [= *Barkleyanthus salicifolius*]	
	Wyethia sp.	Wyethia; Mule's ears
Berberidaceae	*Berberis aquifolium* [=*Mahonia aquifolium*] *Berberis dictyota* [=*Berberis aquifolium* var. *dictyota*; *Berberis californica*; *Mahonia dictyota*]	Oregon grape

PLANT FAMILY	SCIENTIFIC NAME	COMMON NAMES
Boraginaceae	*Amsinckia menziesii* var. *intermedia* [= *Amsinckia intermedia*]	Menzies fiddleneck; Intermediate fiddleneck
	Cryptantha sp.	Cryptantha
	Hackelia patens	Spotted stickseed
	Mertensia sp.	Mountain bluebell
Brassicaceae	*Brassica* sp.	Mustard
	Cardamine concatenata	Cutleaf toothwort; Cutleaf bittercress
	Raphanus sativus	Radish
	Sisymbrium irio	London rocket
Capparaceae	*Isomeris arborea* [= *Cleome isomeris*]	Bladderpod spiderflower
Caprifoliaceae	*Lonicera* sp.	Honeysuckle
	Viburnum sp.	Viburnum
Caryophyllaceae	*Stellaria media*	Common chickweed
Ericaceae	*Arbutus menziesii*	Pacific madrone; Arbutus
	Arctostaphylos tomentosa subsp. *crustacea* [= *A. crustacea*; *A. glandulosa* var. *campbellae*]	Brittleleaf manzanita
	Arctostaphylos pringlei subsp. *drupacea*	Pink-bracted manzanita
	Arctostaphylos glauca	Bigberry manzanita
	Arctostaphylos patula	Greenleaf manzanita
	Pieris japonica [= *Andromeda japonica*]	
Fabaceae	*Astragalus lentiginosus*	Specklepod milkvetch
	Cercis occidentalis	Western redbud
	Cytisus scoparius	Scotch broom
	Lotus scoparius	Western bird's foot trefoil
	Lupinus albifrons	Whiteleaf bush lupine
	Lupinus bicolor	Miniature lupine
	Trifolium repens	White clover

PLANT FAMILY	SCIENTIFIC NAME	COMMON NAMES
	Vicia americana [= *Vicia californica*]	American vetch
Fagaceae	*Castanea* sp.	Chestnut
	Quercus sp.	Oak
Geraniaceae	*Geranium* sp.	Wild geranium
Grossulariaceae	*Ribes aureum*	Golden currant
	Ribes cereum	Wax currant
	Ribes menziesii	Canyon gooseberry
	Ribes roezlii	Sierra gooseberry
	Ribes velutinum	Desert gooseberry
	Ribes viscosissimum	Sticky currant
Hydrophyllaceae	*Eriodictyon* sp.	Yerba Santa
	Nemophila heterophylla [= *Nemophila exilis*]	Variable nemophila
	Nemophila menziesii	Menzies' baby blue-eyes
	Phacelia cicutaria	Caterpillar phacelia; Caterpillar scorpionweed
	Phacelia distans	Distant phacelia; Distant scorpionweed
	Phacelia heterophylla	Variable phacelia; Variable scorpionweed
	Pholistoma auritum	Blue fiesta flower
Lamiaceae	*Glechoma hederacea*	Ground ivy
	Salvia carduacea	Thistle sage
	Salvia mellifera	Black sage
Liliaceae	*Erythronium albidum*	White fawn lily
	Erythronium americanum	American fawn lily
Limnanthaceae	*Limnanthes douglasii*	Douglas' meadowfoam
Oxalidaceae	*Oxalis* sp.	Oxalis; Woodsorrel
Papaveraceae	*Dicentra* sp.	Dicentra; Bleeding heart
	Eschscholzia californica	California poppy
Plumbaginaceae	*Armeria* sp.	Thrift; Sea pink
Polemoniaceae	*Gilia tricolor*	Bird's eyes

PLANT FAMILY	SCIENTIFIC NAME	COMMON NAMES
	Polemonium sp.	Polemonium; Jacob's Ladder
Portulacaceae	*Claytonia lanceolata*	Spring beauty
	Montia fontana [= *Montia hallii*]	Water chickweed; Blinks
Ranunculaceae	*Ranunculus californicus*	California buttercup
Rhamnaceae	*Ceanothus integerrimus*	Deer brush
	Rhamnus betulifolia [= *Frangula betulifolia*]	Birchleaf buckthorn; Birchleaf false buckthorn
	Rhamnus californica	California coffeeberry
	Rhamnus crocea	Spiny redberry
Rosaceae	*Adenostoma fasciculatum*	Chamise; Common chamise
	Amelanchier sp.	Serviceberry
	Cercocarpus montanus [= *C. betulaefolius*]	Birchleaf mountain mahogany
	Fallugia sp.	Apache plume
	Fragaria sp.	Strawberry
	Prunus subcordata	Klamath plum
	Rosa sp.	Wild rose
	Rubus discolor	Himalayan blackberry
	Rubus ursinus	California blackberry
Rutaceae	*Zanthoxylum* sp.	Prickly ash
Salicaceae	*Salix laevigata*	Red willow; Polished willow
Scrophulariaceae	*Collinsia heterophylla*	Chinese houses; Harlequin blue-eyed mary
	Mimulus sp.	Monkey flower
	Penstemon cyaneus	Platte River penstemon; Blue penstemon
	Penstemon humilis	Low penstemon
Solanaceae	*Lycium* sp.	Lycium; Wolfberry; Desert thorn; Matrimony vine
Tamaricaceae	*Tamarix* sp.	Tamarix
Thymelaeaceae	*Dirca* sp.	Leatherwood
Violaceae	*Viola* sp.	Violet

Bibliography

This bibliographical list includes most of the published work on the biology and management of the blue orchard bee, *Osmia lignaria*. It also includes references of those studies on other managed *Osmia* and *Megachile* that report on results or observations mentioned in different sections of this book.

Anderson JL, and Torchio PF. 1989. Potential of blue orchard bees as fruit pollinators. Proc. Utah Hort. Assoc. 12: 1–4.

Baker EW. 1962. Natural history of Plummers Island, Maryland. XV. Descriptions of the stages of *Chaetodactylus krombeini*, new species, a mite associated with the bee *Osmia lignaria* Say. Proc. Biol. Soc. Wash. 75: 227–236.

Batra SWT. 1979. *Osmia cornifrons* and *Pithitis smaragdula*, two Asian bees introduced into the United States for crop pollination. Proc. IVth Int. Symp. on Pollination. Md. Agric. Exp. Sta. Spec. Misc. Publ. 1: 307–312.

Batra SWT. 1998. Hornfaced bees for apple pollination. Am. Bee J. 138: 364–365.

Bekey R, and Klostermeyer EC. 1981. Orchard mason bee. Washington State University. Extension Bulletin No. 922.

Bosch J. 1994. Improvement of field management of *Osmia cornuta* (Latreille) (Hymenoptera, Megachilidae). Apidologie 25: 71–83.

Bosch J. 1994. The nesting behaviour of the mason bee, *Osmia cornuta*

(Latr) with special reference to its pollinating potential (Hymenoptera, Megachilidae). Apidologie 25: 84–93.

Bosch J, and Kemp WP. 1999. Exceptional cherry production in an orchard pollinated with blue orchard bees. Bee World 80: 163–173.

Bosch J, and Kemp WP. 2000. Development and emergence of the orchard pollinator *Osmia lignaria* (Hymenoptera: Megachilidae). Environ. Entomol. 29: 8–13.

Bosch J, and Kemp WP. 2000. Developmental biology and rearing methods for *Osmia* bees used as crop pollinators. In: Pollination in Greenhouses. Sommeijer MJ, and de Ruijter A (eds.). CIP–DATA Koninklijke Bibliotheek, Den Haag.

Bosch J, and Kemp WP. 2001. Developing and establishing bee species as crop pollinators: the example of *Osmia* spp. (Hymenoptera: Megachilidae) and fruit trees. Bull. Ent. Res. (in press)

Bosch J, Kemp WP, and Peterson SS. 2000. Management of *Osmia lignaria* (Hymenoptera: Megachilidae) populations for almond pollination: methods to advance bee emergence. Environ. Entomol. 29: 874–883.

Bosch J, Maeta Y, and Rust RW. 2001. A phylogenetic analysis of nesting behavior in the genus *Osmia* (Hymenoptera: Megachilidae). Ann. Entomol. Soc. Am. 94: 617–627.

Cripps C, and Rust RW. 1989. Pollen preferences of seven *Osmia* species (Hymenoptera: Megachilidae). Environ. Entomol. 18: 133–138.

Cripps C, and Rust RW. 1989. Pollen foraging in a community of *Osmia* bees (Hymenoptera: Megachilidae). Environ. Entomol. 18: 582–589.

Eves JD. 1970. Biology of *Monodontomerus obscurus* Westwood, a parasite of the alfalfa leafcutting bee, *Megachile rotundata* (Fabricius) (Hymenoptera: Torymidae; Megachilidae). Melanderia 4: 1–18.

Eves JD, Mayer DF, and Johansen CA. 1980. Parasites, predators and nest destroyers of the alfalfa leafcutting bee, *Megachile rotundata*. Washington State University, Agric. Exp. Stn. Pullman, WA, Western Regional Extension Publication No. 32.

Fauria K, and Campan R. 1998. Do solitary bees *Osmia cornuta* Latr. and *Osmia lignaria* Cresson use proximal cues to localize their nest? J. Insect Behav. 11: 649–669.

Griffin BL. 1999. The orchard mason bee. Knox Cellars Publishing. Bellingham, WA. 128 pp.

Jahns TR, and Jolliff GD. 1991. Survival rate and reproductive success of *Osmia lignaria propinqua* Cresson (Hymenoptera: Megachilidae) in caged meadowfoam, *Limnanthes alba* Benth. (Limnanthaceae). J. Kansas Entomol. Soc. 64: 95–106.

Jahns TR, and Jolliff GD. 1991. *Osmia lignaria propinqua* Cresson: an alternative pollinator for meadowfoam in cages. Crop Science 31: 1274–1279.

Klostermeyer EC. 1979. *Osmia lignaria* as a fruit tree pollinator in Washington state. Proc. IVth Int. Symp. on Pollination. Md. Agric. Exp. Sta. Spec. Misc. Publ. 1: 295–298.

Krombein KV. 1962. Natural history of Plummers Island, Maryland. XVI. Biological notes on *Chaetodactylus krombeini* Baker, a parasitic mite of the megachilid bee *Osmia (Osmia) lignaria* Say (Acarina: Chaetodactylidae). Proc. Biol. Soc. Wash. 75: 237–249.

Krombein KV. 1967. Trap-nesting wasps and bees: life histories, nests and associates. Smithsonian, Washington DC. 570 pp.

Kuhn ED, and Ambrose JT. 1984. Pollination of 'Delicious' apple by megachilid bees of the genus *Osmia* (Hymenoptera: Megachilidae). J. Kansas Entomol. Soc. 57: 169–180.

Levin MD. 1957. Artificial nesting burrows for *Osmia lignaria* Say. J. Econ. Ent. 50: 506–507.

Levin MD. 1966. Biological notes on *Osmia lignaria* and *Osmia californica* (Hymenoptera: Apoidea, Megachilidae). J. Kansas Entomol. Soc. 39: 524–535.

Levin MD, and Haydak MH. 1957. Comparative value of different pollens in the nutrition of *Osmia lignaria* Say. Bee World 38: 221–226.

Linsley EG, and MacSwain JW. 1941. The bionomics of *Ptinus californicus*, a depredator in the nests of bees. Bull. So. Calif. Acad. Sci. 49: 126–137.

Linsley EG, and MacSwain JW. 1943. Observations on the life history of *Trichodes ornatus* (Coleoptera, Cleridae), a larval predator in the nests of bees and wasps. Ann. Entomol. Soc. Am. 36: 549–601.

Linsley EG, and MacSwain JW. 1951. Notes on the biology of *Tricrania stansburyi* Haldeman (Coleoptera, Meloidae). Bull. So. Calif. Acad. Sci. 50: 92–95.

Maeta Y. 1988. Nest structure and natural enemies of *Osmia lignaria lignaria* Say (Hymenoptera, Megachilidae). Chugoku Kontyu 2: 1–8. [In Japanese]

Maeta Y. 1990. Utilization of wild bees. Farming Japan 24: 13–19.

Maeta Y, and Kitamura T. 1968. Some biological notes on the introduced wild bee *Osmia (Osmia) lignaria* Say (Hymenoptera: Megachilidae) Bull. Tohoku Natl. Agric. Exp. Stn. 36: 53–70.

Maeta Y, and Kitamura T. 1974. How to manage the Mame-ko bee (*Osmia cornifrons* Radoszkowski) for pollination of fruit crops. Ask. Co. Ltd. 16 pp. [In Japanese]

Maeta Y, and Kitamura T. 1981. Pollinating efficiency by *Osmia cornifrons*

(Radoszkowski) in relation to required number of nesting bees for economic fruit production. Honeybee Sci. 2: 65–72. [In Japanese]

Phillips JK, and Klostermeyer EC. 1978. Nesting behavior of *Osmia lignaria propinqua* Cresson (Hymenoptera: Megachilidae). J. Kans. Entomol. Soc. 51: 91–108.

Rau P. 1937. The life history of *Osmia lignaria* and *O. cordata*, with notes on *O. conjuncta*. Ann. Ent. Soc. Amer. 30: 324–343.

Rust RW. 1974. The systematics and biology of the genus *Osmia*, subgenera *Osmia, Chalcosmi*a and *Cephalosmia* (Hymenoptera: Megachilidae). Wasmann J. Biol. 32: 1–93.

Rust RW. 1987. Collecting of *Pinus* (Pinaceae) pollen by *Osmia* (Hymenoptera: Megachilidae). Environ. Entomol. 16: 668–671.

Rust RW. 1990. Spatial and temporal heterogeneity of pollen foraging in *Osmia lignaria propinqua* (Hymenoptera: Megachilidae). Environ. Entomol. 19: 332–338.

Rust RW. 1991. Size–weight relationships in *Osmia lignaria propinqua* Cresson (Hymenoptera: Megachilidae). J. Kansas Entomol. Soc. 64: 174–178.

Rust RW. 1993. Cell and nest construction costs in two cavity-nesting bees (*Osmia lignaria propinqua* and *Osmia ribifloris biedermannii*) (Hymenoptera: Megachilidae). Ann. Entomol. Soc. Am. 86: 327–332.

Rust RW. 1995. Adult overwinter mortality in *Osmia lignaria propinqua* Cresson (Hymenoptera: Megachilidae). Pan–Pac. Entomol. 71: 121–124.

Rust RW, and Torchio PF. 1991. Induction and incidence of *Ascosphaera* infections in the blue orchard bee, *Osmia lignaria propinqua* (Hymenoptera: Megachilidae). Acta Horticulturae 288: 169–172.

Rust RW, and Torchio PF. 1991. Induction of *Ascosphaera* (Ascomycetes: Ascosphaerales) infections in field populations of *Osmia lignaria propinqua* Cresson (Hymenoptera: Megachilidae). Pan-Pac. Entomol. 67: 251–257.

Rust RW, and Torchio PF. 1992. Effects of temperature and host developmental stage on *Ascosphaera torchioi* Youssef and McManus prevalence in *Osmia lignaria propinqua* Cresson (Hymenoptera: Megachilidae). Apidologie 23: 1–9.

Tepedino VJ, and Torchio PF. 1982. Phenotypic variability in the nesting success among *Osmia lignaria propinqua* females in a glasshouse environment (Hymenoptera: Megachilidae). Ecol. Entomol. 7: 453–462.

Tepedino VJ, and Torchio PF. 1982. Temporal variability in the sex ratio of a non–social bee, *Osmia lignaria propinqua*: extrinsic determination or the tracking of an optimum? Oikos 38: 177–182.

Tepedino VJ, and Torchio PF. 1989. The influence of nest-hole selection on sex ratio and progeny size in *Osmia lignaria propinqua* (Hymenoptera: Megachilidae). Ann. Entomol. Soc. Am. 82: 355–360.

Tepedino VJ, and Torchio PF. 1994. Founding and usurping: equally efficient paths to nesting success in *Osmia lignaria propinqua* (Hymenoptera: Megachilidae). Ann. Entomol. Soc. Am. 87: 946–953.

Tepedino VJ, Thompson R, and Torchio PF. 1984. Heritability for size in the megachilid bee *Osmia lignaria propinqua* Cresson. Apidologie 15: 83–88.

Torchio PF. 1963. A chalcid wasp parasite of the alfalfa leaf-cutting bee. Farm and Home Science 24: 70–71.

Torchio PF. 1972. *Sapyga pumila* Cresson, a parasite of *Megachile rotundata* (F.) (Hymenoptera: Sapygidae, Megachilidae) II. Methods for control. Melanderia 10: 23–30.

Torchio PF. 1976. Use of *Osmia lignaria* Say (Hymenoptera: Apoidea: Megachilidae) as a pollinator in an apple and prune orchard. J. Kansas Entomol. Soc. 49: 475–482.

Torchio PF. 1979. An eight-year field study involving control of *Sapyga pumila* Cresson (Hymenoptera: Sapygidae), a wasp parasite of the alfalfa leafcutting bee, *Megachile pacifica* Panzer. J. Kansas Entomol. Soc. 52: 412–419.

Torchio PF. 1979. Use of *Osmia lignaria* Say as a pollinator of caged almond in California. Proc. IVth Int. Symp. on Pollination. Md. Agric. Exp. Sta. Spec. Misc. Publ. 1: 285–293.

Torchio PF. 1980. Factors affecting cocoon orientation in *Osmia lignaria propinqua* Cresson (Hymenoptera: Megachilidae). J. Kansas Entomol. Soc. 53: 386–400.

Torchio PF. 1981. Field experiments with *Osmia lignaria propinqua* Cresson as a pollinator in almond orchards: I, 1975 studies (Hymenoptera: Megachilidae). J. Kansas Entomol. Soc. 54: 815–823.

Torchio PF. 1981. Field experiments with *Osmia lignaria propinqua* Cresson as a pollinator in almond orchards: II, 1976 studies (Hymenoptera: Megachilidae). J. Kansas Entomol. Soc. 54: 824–836.

Torchio PF. 1982. Field experiments with *Osmia lignaria propinqua* Cresson as a pollinator in almond orchards: III, 1977 studies (Hymenoptera: Megachilidae). J. Kansas Entomol. Soc. 55: 101–116.

Torchio PF. 1982. Field experiments with the pollinator species, *Osmia lignaria propinqua* Cresson in apple orchards: I, 1975 studies (Hymenoptera: Megachilidae). J. Kansas Entomol. Soc. 55: 136–144.

Torchio PF. 1982. Field experiments with the pollinator species, *Osmia lignaria propinqua* Cresson in apple orchards: II, 1976 studies (Hymenoptera: Megachilidae). J. Kansas Entomol. Soc. 55: 759–778.

Torchio PF. 1984. Field experiments with the pollinator species, *Osmia lignaria propinqua* Cresson (Hymenoptera: Megachilidae) in apple orchards: III, 1977 studies. J. Kansas Entomol. Soc. 57: 517–521.

Torchio PF. 1984. Field experiments with the pollinator species, *Osmia lignaria propinqua* Cresson (Hymenoptera: Megachilidae) in apple orchards: IV, 1978 studies. J. Kansas Entomol. Soc. 57: 689–694.

Torchio PF. 1985. Field experiments with the pollinator species, *Osmia lignaria propinqua* Cresson in apple orchards: V, (1979–1980), methods of introducing bees, nesting success, seed counts, fruit yields (Hymenoptera: Megachilidae). J. Kansas Entomol. Soc. 58: 448–464.

Torchio PF. 1987. Use of non-honey bee species as pollinators of crops. Proc. Ent. Soc. Ont. 118:111–124.

Torchio PF. 1988. The blue orchard bee: an alternative pollinator of apples. Utah Science 49: 2–9.

Torchio PF. 1989. In-nest biologies and immature development of three *Osmia* species (Hymenoptera: Megachilidae). Ann. Entomol. Soc. Am. 82: 599–615.

Torchio PF. 1989. Biology, immature development, and adaptive behavior of *Stelis montana*, a cleptoparasite of *Osmia* spp. (Hymenoptera: Megachilidae). Ann. Entomol. Soc. Am. 82: 616–632.

Torchio PF. 1991. Bees as crop pollinators and the role of solitary species in changing environments. Acta Horticulturae 288: 49–61.

Torchio PF. 1991. Use of *Osmia lignaria propinqua* (Hymenoptera: Megachilidae) as a mobile pollinator of orchard crops. Environ. Entomol. 20: 590–596.

Torchio PF. 1992. Effects of dosage and temperature on pathogenic expressions of chalkbrood syndrome caused by *Ascosphaera torchioi* within larvae of *Osmia lignaria propinqua* (Hymenoptera: Megachilidae). Environ. Entomol. 21: 1086–1091.

Torchio PF, and Asensio E. 1985. The introduction of the European bee, *Osmia cornuta* Latr., into the U.S as a potential pollinator of orchard crops, and a comparison of its manageability with *Osmia lignaria propinqua* Cresson (Hymenoptera: Megachilidae). J. Kansas Entomol. Soc. 58: 42–52.

Torchio PF, and Bosch J. 1992. Biology of *Tricrania stansburyi*, a meloid beetle cleptoparasite of the bee *Osmia lignaria propinqua* (Hymenoptera: Megachilidae). Ann. Entomol. Soc. Am. 85: 713–721.

Torchio PF, and Tepedino VJ. 1980. Sex ratio, body size and seasonality in a solitary bee, *Osmia lignaria propinqua* (Hymenoptera: Megachilidae). Evolution 34: 993–1003.

Vicens N, Bosch J. 2000. Pollinating efficacy of *Osmia cornuta* and *Apis mellifera* (Hymenoptera: Megachilidae, Apidae) on 'Red Delicious' apple. Environ. Entomol. 29: 235–240.

Williams NM, Goodell K. 2000. The association of mandible shape and nesting material in *Osmia* Panzer (Hymenoptera: Megachilidae): a morphometric analysis. Ann. Entomol. Soc. Am. 93: 318–325.

Yamada M. 1990. Control of *Chaetodactylus* mite, *Chaetodactylus nipponicus* Kurosa, an important mortality agent of hornfaced bee, *Osmia cornifrons* Radoszkowski. Bull. Aomori Apple Exp. Stn. 26: 39–77. [In Japanese]

Youssef NN, McManus WR, and Torchio PF. 1985. Cross-infectivity potential of *Ascosphaera* spp. (Ascomycetes: *Ascosphaera*) on the bee *Osmia lignaria propinqua* Cresson. J. Econ. Entomol. 78: 227–231.

Youssef NN, and McManus WR. *Ascosphaera torchioi* sp. nov., a pathogen of *Osmia lignaria propinqua* Cresson (Hymenoptera). Mycotaxon 77: 7–13.

Index

Absconding 24, 42, 43, 45, 46
Adult 11, 27
Adulthood 9, 27, 28, 30, 31, 40
Aging 25
Alfalfa leafcutting bee vi, 54, 58, 62
Almonds 2, 14, 39
Alternative pollen-nectar sources 36, 41
Anthrenus 59
Ants 63
    protection against 26, 63
Apples 2, 14, 73
Argentine ants 63
Ascosphaera 62, 64
    protection against 62
Ascosphaerales 62
Attagenus 59

Birds 63, 68
    protection against 23, 24, 63
Black light traps 51, 52
Blister beetle 56
BOB
    appearance 4, 6
    coexistence with honey bees 72
    gentleness 3, 5
    geographic distribution 5

BOB *continued*
    ranching (or farming) 41, 42, 67, 73
    suppliers 69, 70
Body size 10, 70
    and cell size 11, 65
    and mortality 39, 47
    and provision size 7, 8
    and sex 4, 6, 8, 65

Cap 8
Cardboard tubes 18, 26, 50
Carpet beetles 59, 60
Cell(s)
    per nest 8, 9, 65, 70
    position and progeny sex 7, 8, 11, 65
    production 8, 44
    production rates 25, 46
    size and progeny sex 7, 8, 11, 65
Chaetodactylidae 59
Chaetodactylus krombeini 59, 61, 64
    protection against 62
Chaetodactylus nipponicus 62
Chalcid wasps 49, 51, 53
Chalkbrood 37, 64
Checkered flower beetle 57
    trap 57, 58

Cherry 2, 15, 73
   yields 15
Chickweed 42
Choke cherry 42
Chrysididae 54
Chrysidid wasps 54
Chrysura 53, 54
Cleptoparasites 54, 55, 56, 59
Cleridae 57
Cocoon 10
   inserted 37
   reversed 26
   spinning 10, 26, 27, 29
Crabapples 42
Crows 63
Cuckoo bee 55
Custom pollination 73

Dandelions 12, 36, 42
Dermestidae 59
Development 9, 10, 22, 25, 26, 27
   checks 9, 26, 28
   monitoring 9, 26, 28, 29, 30
Developmental mortality 29, 39, 46, 47, 70
Diseases 38, 70, 72
Dispersal 7, 35, 37, 38, 39, 40, 44, 45, 72
Drift 38

Egg
   appearance 7, 10, 27
   fertilization and progeny sex 8
   laying 8
   mortality 23, 25, 43, 46, 68
Emergence 5, 9, 48
   advancing 39
   box 37
   checks 9, 33, 36
   delaying 33
   period 22, 25, 28, 29, 31, 32, 33, 39, 40, 47, 70
   temperature 33, 34, 36
   timing with bloom 31, 32, 33, 35, 36, 39, 40, 45, 72
   during wintering 31, 33, 47
Establishment 25, 38, 44

Eulophidae 51
Extended flowering periods 41, 42

Fat body 30, 31, 40
Flour beetles 59
Flower-visiting records 12, 74
Flying period 5, 70
Foraging behavior 12
Foraging range 38
Feces 10, 27
Fire ants 63
Fruit tree
   alternate bearing 39
   fertilization 2
   flower development 9, 36
   flowering periods 1, 35
   pollination 1, 35, 38
   weather during bloom 1, 15, 38, 72
   yields 2, 15, 35
Fungicides 45

Generations per year 5, 9
Geographic origin
   and development 11, 12, 29, 30, 31, 32, 40, 47, 72
Gregarious behavior 4, 7
Grooved boards 16, 19

Hairy-fingered mite 37, 59
Honey bee vi, 3, 15, 62, 72, 73
Honey stomach (or crop) 7
Hornfaced bee vi, 3, 62
Humidity
   and development 26, 29

Incubation 9, 22, 32, 33, 34, 36, 37, 39
   box 36, 37
   temperature 33
Inter-cavity space 21
Insecticides 45

King blossom 2, 3

Landmarks 23, 43
Larva 10, 27
Leucospidae 53
Leucospis affinis 52, 53

Leucospis affinis continued
    protection against 21, 53
Life cycle 9, 40
Linepithema humile 63
Logan Bee Lab web site 16
Longevity 8, 25
Loose cocoons 37, 39, 61, 63

Mass release 37
Mating 5, 6, 36
Meadowfoam 42
Meconium 12
Megachile rotundata 54
Megachilidae 4, 55
Megatoma 59
Melittobia chalybii 51, 52
Meloidae 56
Metabolic rates 30
Metabolic reserves 30, 47
Mice 63
    protection against 23, 26, 63
Milk cartons 18, 50
Mites 37, 59, 61, 64
Monodontomerus 49, 52
    protection against 50, 52
Mud
    collection 7, 8
    sources 9, 24
Mustards 42

Natal nests 37, 39, 44, 72
Natural nesting sites 6, 67
Nest appearance 7, 11
Nest cavity
    dimensions 16, 20, 71
    new vs. old 38, 63
    number per female 35, 38
    selection 6
Nest inspection 17, 18, 19, 20, 61, 71
Nesting behavior 5
Nesting blocks 16, 17
Nesting boxes 16, 18, 50
Nesting materials 16, 71
    color 16
    distribution 35, 38
    orientation 25
    relocation 24, 46

Nesting materials *continued*
    retrieving 9, 25
    sanitation 63
    setting up 9, 23
    suppliers 16
    types 16
    waterproofing 17
Nesting period 9, 22, 23, 25
Nesting shelters 23, 24
Night station traps 54, 55

Oregon grape 42
Orientation flights 6
Osmia californica 68
Osmia cornifrons vi, 14, 62
Osmia cornuta vii, 15
Osmia lignaria 4
    subspecies 5

Paper straws 17, 26
Parasites 9, 17, 18, 19, 20, 21, 25, 26,
    29, 38, 49, 68, 70, 72
    introduction to new areas 70
Pathogens 49, 62
Pears 2
Peromyscus 63
Pesticides 41, 42, 45, 46
    sublethal doses 45
Plastic straws 17
Plug 7, 8, 11
Pollen mites 59
Pollen sources 12, 13
Pollen-nectar collection 7, 8
Pollinating efficacy 12
Population
    density for optimal pollination 14,
        35, 38
    growth 44
    increases or returns 15, 66, 72
    moving or relocating 41, 42, 46
    quantifying 9, 65
    shipment 69
    size per acre 14, 35, 38
Predators 9, 25, 29, 49, 63, 68, 70, 72
Prepupa 11, 27
Prepupal developmental arrest 27, 29,
    30, 47, 66

Prepupal dormancy 11, 30, 47
Pre-nesting period 6, 36
Pre-wintering 9, 22, 25, 28, 30, 31, 40
Provision 7, 8
    and flower visits 7
    and humidity 46
    and mold 46
    and nectar 39, 46
    size 7, 8
    small 39, 46
Ptinidae 58
Ptinus californicus 58, 60
Pupa 11, 27
Purchasing BOBs 69
    regulations 69

Rearing 22, 62, 66, 70, 72
    artificial conditions 22, 26, 27, 29, 40
    calendar 9, 22, 26
    natural conditions 22, 26, 27, 29, 40
Reeds 16, 20, 50
Release 9, 32, 35, 36, 37, 44, 72
Robins 63
Rodents 63, 68

Sapyga 53, 54
    control against 54, 55
Sapygidae 54
Sapygid wasps 54
Scavengers 58, 59
Sciurus griseus 63
Scopa 5, 6, 7
Sex ratio 8, 9, 39, 65, 66, 70
    and cavity dimensions 20
Social bees 4
Solenopsis invicta 63
Solid blocks 16
Solitary bees 4
Solitary wasps 68
Spider beetle 58
Spermatheca 8
Split release 37
Squirrels 63
Starlings 63
Stelis montana 55, 56
Sticky barriers 63
Styrene blocks 18

Summer dormancy 11
Summer storage 9, 25, 26, 28

Temperature
    and development 27, 29, 66
    and foraging activity 14, 37
    and wintering 31, 40, 47
    fluctuating vs. constant 27, 30, 40, 47
Tenebrionidae 59
Torymidae 49
Trap-nesting 67
    regulations 69
Trap-nests 68
Tribolium 59, 61
Trichodes ornatus 57
    protection against 57, 58
Tricrania stansburyi 56
Triungulin 56
Trogoderma 59, 60

Ultraviolet light traps 51
Uncapped nests 50
Unmated females 8, 70
Unsealed cells 58, 59

Vestibular cell 7, 8, 11
Vigor 25, 30, 33, 45, 48, 72

Wafer boards 19
Weather
    and foraging activity 1, 14, 38, 70, 72, 73
    and pollination 1, 15, 38, 72
    and population release 9, 36, 37
Wild bees
    population declines 1, 67
Willows 36, 42
Winter mortality 47, 66
    and temperature 29
Winter storage 9
Wintering 9, 11, 22, 25, 28, 30, 31, 32, 39, 70
    duration 31, 33, 39, 40
    temperature 31, 40, 47
Wood blocks 17
Woodpeckers 63

X-rays 27, 28, 30, 66